C408654332

D0854495

Antony Worrall Thompson's Top 100 Beef Recipes

To David Wilby and his team of chefs at Notting Grill,
Kew Grill and the Angel Coaching Inn and Grill

antony worrall thompson's top **100**

BEEF recipes

Quick and easy dishes for every occasion

BOOKS

Contents

Introduction

Those of us who eat beef don't just like it, we love it. Beef has certainly had its problems over the last 10–15 years through BSE and foot-and-mouth disease, and its popularity definitely declined. Well, the great news is that new rules and regulations mean that British beef is now probably the safest in the world. Once again we can publicly enjoy this great red meat that is part of our heritage; the very reason the French gave us the nickname 'Les Rosbifs'.

I was so convinced that the public wanted a return to beef that I opened Notting Grill restaurant in London, despite objections from my wife and Operations Director. Luckily for me I was right. Two years later, Notting Grill is a thriving business and we've since opened two more: the Angel Coaching Inn and Grill at Heytesbury near Warminster in Wiltshire, and Kew Grill, near Kew Gardens in Surrey.

As a customer I yearned for a really good steak, and yet, apart from one or two restaurants in London, I couldn't think of where to find one. Most restaurants served fillet steak, usually smothered in sauce, but I wanted a plain rump, rib or sirloin with just a little Béarnaise sauce on the side – a combination that will never date.

The first challenge for me was to find the best meat. British beef may be safe, but not all of it is of the quality I demand. It should have good marbling, which is the little rivulets of fat embracing the red eye or muscles of the beast. The fat on the outside should be of a decent thickness and should be a yellowish colour, indicating that the steer has been fed on grass or grass silage and not too much barley, which creates a white fat and in my opinion toughens the muscle, giving it much tighter fibres.

The process of ageing beef is very important for tenderness and flavour. Ageing beef is a chemical change that happens under controlled temperatures. The first 11 days are all about tenderizing the meat, while the following days, during which the meat is hung, are very much to do with flavour intensity. As the meat dehydrates and shrinks, the flavour is strengthened, giving that old-fashioned beefy taste that is so rarely found today.

Buying beef of any age is difficult in a time when butchers can no longer afford the time to hang beef. For the most part, supermarkets have replaced local butchers, and in doing so they've lost the skills that artisan butchers brought to the party. For some reason, super-markets believe that customers want bright red meat with very white fat – they even install lights that enhance the redness! I, on the other hand, want beef that's almost purple in colour with a fine coating of yellow fat. However, ageing beef ties up meat-holding space, and the fact that the meat shrinks by 13–25 per cent during the process means that it costs the customer more, a policy supermarkets are reluctant to pursue as so much of their marketing is based on cost-cutting and competing with other supermarket chains.

Before we discuss steaks and prime cuts, there is the rest of the beast to consider (see illustration overleaf). The beauty of cuts nearer the neck or nearer the ground is that although they may be tougher and take longer to cook, they contain real flavour. One of the reasons steak is so expensive is that not enough people buy the cheaper cuts – the perfect braising and stewing meats that taste delicious, even though a little more effort is required to achieve a great result. A lovely stew or braised meat is one of life's little pleasures, especially on colder days. The very act of braising or stewing involves browning the meat, then adding some flavourings such as vegetables and herbs, then a liquid content which could be wine, stock, water or a combination of all three. The liquid is brought to the boil and the heat is reduced so that the surface of the liquid merely 'burps'. Then the pan is covered tightly to prevent evaporation, which promotes both poaching and steaming. This can be done on the top of the stove or in a slow oven. The latter is a less intense method of cooking, enabling the meat to cook for a longer period of time, becoming tender without burning. Boiling stew will make the meat dry and hard.

Mince (ground beef) tends to be the value cut of choice, used for bolognese sauce, shepherd's pie or burgers. There is a common misconception about beef mince that it is quick to cook; a lot of people think you can throw some mince into a pot and knock up a bolognese in 30 minutes. It is forgotten that mince generally comes from very tough cuts of meat and as such should be cooked slowly over a long period of time.

Pure mince burgers cooked for a short period of time don't do it for me; they remain tough and often fairly tasteless. At my restaurants we only mince the trimmings from prime cuts – fillet, sirloin, rump and rib – that have been well hung, giving the burgers a magnificent flavour. Hanging meat at home is not recommended, however, as the bacteria that collect on a single steak can cause illness. We hang large cuts and are able to trim the outside to remove the problem.

One area this book doesn't tackle is offal (variety meats). Apart from steak and kidney, I don't believe many people will cook with beef liver, heart, tripe and so on as they are too strong for our modern tastebuds.

Brisket

Fillet (Tenderloin)

Fore Rib (Rib-eye)

Chuck

Leg (Shank)

Silverside (Bottom Round)

Thick Flank (Round Tip)

Thick Rib (Rib Roast)

Topside (Top Round)

Neck

Rump

Sirloin

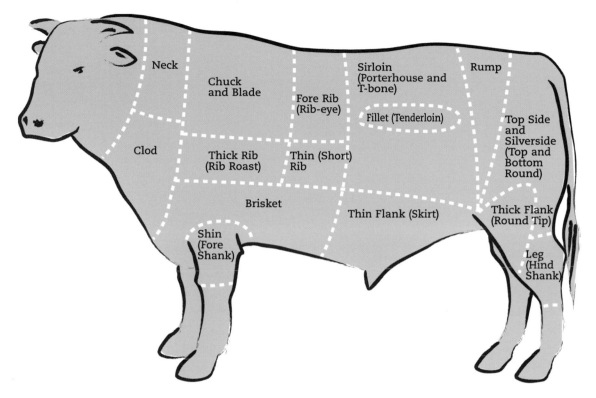

Neck

Chuck and Blade

Fore Rib (Rib-eye)

Sirloin (Porterhouse and T-bone)

Rump

Fillet (Tenderloin)

Top Side and Silverside (Top and Bottom Round)

Clod

Thick Rib (Rib Roast)

Thin (Short) Rib

Brisket

Thin Flank (Skirt)

Thick Flank (Round Tip)

Shin (Fore Shank)

Leg (Hind Shank)

Notes for cooks in America, Australia and New Zealand

Cup measurements and terms, which are used by cooks in America, Australia and New Zealand appear in brackets where necessary. All the recipes in this book list both metric and imperial measurements. Conversions are approximate and have been rounded up or down. Follow one set of measurements only; do not mix the two. You can also use kitchen scales to measure dry/solid ingredients. Liquid measurements vary according to country, but remember that an American pint is only 16 fluid ounces whereas an imperial pint is 20 fluid ounces. All pints listed in this book are imperial. Tablespoon sizes in this book are UK/US, so Australian readers should measure 3 teaspoons where 1 tablespoon is specified. You may find this list useful:

4 fl oz (125 ml) = ½ cup
8 fl oz (250 ml) = 1 cup
16 fl oz (450 ml) = 1 US pint
1 UK/AUS pint (20 fl oz) (600 ml) = 2½ cups

1 teaspoon = 5 ml
1 tablespoon (UK/US) = 3 teaspoons = 15 ml
1 tablespoon (AUS) = 4 teaspoons = 20 ml

Some ingredients, methods and kitchen equipment regularly mentioned in this book have different American terms. They are: chillies (chili peppers), cling film (plastic wrap), cocktail stick (toothpick), frying pan (skillet), griddle pan (heavy skillet or cast-iron frying pan), grill (broiler; to grill = to broil), lengthways (lengthwise), muslin (cheesecloth), to whisk (to beat).

I think you'll agree that all beef fans love a good steak, but what constitutes a perfect steak? At Notting Grill, fillet steak tops the list in popularity, customers requiring tenderness at the expense of flavour. For me it's the rib-eye, still quite tender but with enough fat and textures to make for an exciting chew. I used to love a rump but, with rump, you live a little on the edge, never knowing whether its superb flavour is going to be accompanied by a tough, well-used muscle or whether it will melt in the mouth. Sirloin tends to be the compromise steak: not as much flavour as the rib-eye or rump, yet not as tender as the fillet. The ultimate steak for those who have a large appetite is the T-bone: sirloin on one side of the bone, fillet on the other, a balance of flavours and texture but, at 650 g (1 lb 7 oz), one big mouthful.

Steak is all about buying the best-quality meat, and for this you're going to have to pay handsomely. When I see a sign outside a pub reading 'Steak and Chips – £5.50', I wonder about where the meat has come from. At my restaurants it costs me more than that to put a steak on the plate, and that's before the garnish and the chips. Good steak is not cheap, and I believe it's worth eating it a little less often but paying top dollar and enjoying real meat when you do.

The cooking is down to you. Simplicity can be the trickiest form of cookery as the steak has to tell its own story, with no sauce to camouflage a cock-up. The most common mistake made at home is overcooking steak, as the cook often plays it safe – fine if you like your meat well-done, but a waste of money if you like anything rarer than medium. Getting it right depends on several criteria: the thickness of the steak, the cut of the steak, whether it is at room temperature or fridge-cold, and whether the pan or grill has been preheated before cooking.

I always bring the steak to room temperature by removing it from the fridge 30 minutes before I want to cook it. At home I prefer to cook my steaks on a heavy-based griddle pan; grilling the meat doesn't do the steak any favours as domestic grill temperatures are just not hot enough to seal steaks. As an alternative, electric grilling machines have improved enormously over the last few years, and they have the benefit of cooking the meat on both sides at once.

It is hard to use meat thermometers on steak as they tend to be bulky probes and would need to be in the meat throughout the cooking process. For your interest, a steak should ideally reach the following temperatures for the different stages of cooking: 57°C/135°F (rare), 63°C/145°F (medium-rare), 68°C/155°F (medium), 71°C/160°F (medium-well), 74°C/165°F (well done).

It's important to have your pan very hot to start the cooking process. Season the steak with salt and ground black pepper just before cooking. Then sear the steak to brown the surface on both sides, creating a caramelized crust of the juices that come to the surface, giving great texture, colour and flavour.

Without a meat thermometer how do you tell when a steak is cooked? Chefs use the touch test, which will take you a little time to master. This is best described as follows. Using whichever hand you use more regularly, point the fingers upwards, bend your index finger over and touch the triangular piece of flesh between your thumb and index finger on the same hand – it will feel soft, and that's the texture of rare meat. Bring the second finger (next to your index finger) over and touch the same piece of flesh – it will have tightened a little, and that's medium to medium-rare. Using the next finger, the flesh is even tighter, the texture of medium to medium-well done. And if you can get your little finger over to touch the flesh it will feel very tight, and that's how well-done meat feels. It's all in the touch, and it's all about experience... so practise!

This has been an exciting book to write. At first I was a little daunted at the prospect of finding 100 beef recipes, but once I'd looked around the world and discovered a whole palate of flavours, colours and ideas, I could have written 200 recipes. It was hard to know which to leave out. I've given you some classic dishes, perhaps with a little AWT twist, and I've treated you to some great steaks. You'll also find curries and tagines that aren't necessarily traditional to their countries of origin (often for reasons of religion), but which work well using beef.

Putting the recipes into categories was also hard – did I do it on price, or on beef cuts? In the end I settled for meal styles – Soups and starters, Salads and sandwiches, Light lunches, Pasta, rice and noodles, Warming winter dishes, Weekday suppers, Special occasions, and Sauces and accompaniments – each containing recipes that for the most part aren't cheffy, are easy to follow, and most importantly taste delicious.

Simplicity is about buying the best ingredients, ingredients that speak for themselves. I can't stop the modern trend for buying ready-made meals and sauces, but I do hope I can encourage you to get back into beef, get back into cooking and have fun. This book needs use, it needs greasy fingerprints; this one's for you.

Antony Worrall Thompson

1 Hungarian Goulash Soup with Parsley Dumplings

Good-value cut
Preparation and cooking: 3 hours 30 minutes
Serves 8

1 tablespoon vegetable oil

25 g (1 oz) (2 tablespoons) butter

2 onions, finely chopped

1 kg (2 lb 4 oz) shin (shank) of beef, cut into 1 cm (½ inch) cubes

2 teaspoons paprika

1 teaspoon caraway seeds

1 teaspoon fresh thyme leaves

2 cloves garlic, crushed

2 litres (3½ pints) beef stock

2 red peppers (bell peppers), cored, deseeded and diced

3 medium-hot red chillies, deseeded and sliced

1 x 400 g (14 oz) can chopped tomatoes

2 tablespoons tomato purée

900 g (2 lb) floury (starchy) potatoes, peeled and cut into 1 cm (½ inch) cubes

salt and freshly ground black pepper

soured cream, to serve

PARSLEY DUMPLINGS

see method for ingredients

What's nicer than a bowl of really thick, warming soup on a cold winter's day? And with the addition of parsley dumplings this is a meal in its own right.

1 Melt the oil and butter and gently cook the onion for about 8 minutes, until it begins to soften without colouring. Increase the heat and add the meat, browning it on all sides. Sprinkle in the paprika, remove the pan from the heat and stir thoroughly.

2 Return to the heat and stir-fry for a couple of minutes. Add the caraway seeds, thyme and garlic. Add stock to cover, stirring thoroughly. Simmer gently for 2 hours, adding more stock if necessary.

3 Add the peppers, chillies, tomatoes, tomato purée and potatoes to the pan. Mix thoroughly and add more stock to cover, as necessary. Simmer gently for about 30 minutes, until the potatoes are cooked and the meat is tender. Season to taste.

4 Make the parsley dumplings (see below) and place on the surface of the soup. Cover and place in the oven for 35–40 minutes, or until the dumplings have risen and are golden brown. Pour the soup into bowls and top with a dollop of soured cream and a couple of dumplings. Serve with chunks of country bread.

To make the Parsley Dumplings
Preheat the oven to 180°C/350°F/Gas Mark 4. Sift 250 g (9 oz) (2 cups) plain flour (all-purpose flour), 1 teaspoon salt and 2 teaspoons baking powder into a large bowl. Make a well in the centre and add 2 tablespoons olive oil and 4 table-spoons each of chopped fresh flat-leaf parsley and snipped fresh chives. Then, pour in 150 ml (¼ pint) milk and, using a fork, mix to form a soft dough. Place the dough on a lightly floured surface and knead briefly. Divide and shape into 16 teaspoon-sized dumplings.

2 Stuffed Cabbage Leaves in Tomato Sauce

Good-value cut
Preparation and cooking: 2 hours 30 minutes
Serves 6

1 large Savoy cabbage

1 onion, finely chopped

100 g (4 oz) (4–5 slices) smoked bacon, finely chopped

85 g (3 oz) (6 tablespoons) unsalted butter

2 cloves garlic, mashed to a paste with a little salt

1 teaspoon fresh thyme leaves

675 g (1 lb 8 oz) lean minced (ground) beef

3 tablespoons fresh parsley, chopped plus extra to serve

175 g (6 oz) (1 cup) cooked long grain rice

100 g (4 oz) (1 cup) Roquefort cheese, crumbled

3 tablespoons mascarpone cheese

3 tablespoons pinenuts, toasted

1 teaspoon smoked paprika

salt and freshly ground black pepper

12 slices Parma ham

TOMATO SAUCE

see method for ingredients

I created this dish for *Good Food Live*; it reminded me of the stuffed cabbage my mother used to sell in her deli, although I have modernized it with the addition of some Roquefort and mascarpone cheese.

1 Preheat the oven to 180°C/350°F/Gas Mark 4. Remove the tough outer leaves from the cabbage and discard. Then cut out the core and discard. Loosen the leaves, drop them into a pan of boiling water and cook for 3 minutes; you will need about 12 leaves. Drain, refresh in cold water, drain and dry, then set aside.

2 In a frying pan, cook the onion and bacon together in the unsalted butter until soft. Add the garlic and the thyme and cook for another minute. Allow to cool.

3 Place the mince in a large bowl and combine with the onion mix, chopped parsley, rice, Roquefort and mascarpone cheese, pinenuts and paprika, and season to taste.

4 Lay out the cabbage leaves and line each one with a slice of Parma ham. Place a small amount of the meat mixture on each leaf and roll up, folding in the sides. Set aside until ready to cook.

5 Make the tomato sauce (see below). Once you have arranged the rolls with the sauce in a casserole dish or lidded roasting tray, place the dish on the hob, and bring to the boil. Cover, then place in the oven for 1½–2 hours.

6 Place 2 cabbage rolls on each plate with some buttered carrots and mashed potatoes. Strain the sauce and spoon over the cabbage rolls, then sprinkle with the extra chopped parsley.

To make the tomato sauce
Melt 25 g (1 oz) (2 tablespoons) unsalted butter in a frying pan over a low heat. Add 1 finely sliced celery stalk, 1 peeled and thinly sliced carrot, 1 peeled and thinly sliced onion, 1 clove garlic and 1 sprig fresh thyme. Cook for 8 minutes until soft. Place this vegetable mix in the bottom of a casserole dish or lidded roasting tray. Arrange the rolls snugly over the vegetables, then pour 600 ml (1 pint) tomato passata around them. (See step 5.)

3 Beef Satay and Chilli-peanut Sauce

Prime cut
Preparation and cooking: 30 minutes, plus marinating and soaking time
Serves 4

600 g (1 lb 5 oz) rump beef, cut into 32 x 1 cm (½ inch) cubes

MARINADE

8 shallots, finely chopped

6 cloves garlic, peeled and sliced

3 red chillies, sliced

2.5 cm (1 inch) galangal or fresh ginger, peeled and sliced

2 teaspoons ground turmeric

2 teaspoons ground coriander

½ teaspoon black peppercorns

1 tablespoon peanuts, unsalted

1 teaspoon *blachan* (shrimp paste)

pinch of freshly grated nutmeg

2 cloves

2 tablespoons oil

CHILLI-PEANUT SAUCE

for ingredients and method see page 140

I don't know anyone who doesn't like satay. It's a classic Indonesian or Thai nibble, and its great popularity comes from the wonderful balance of flavours. If you haven't time to prepare my delicious Chilli-peanut Sauce you could spice up some shop-bought satay sauce with a little chilli oil.

1 Soak 8 bamboo skewers in cold water for 30 minutes to prevent them from burning. In a bowl, combine all the marinade ingredients except the oil together to form a paste.

2 Heat the oil in a frying pan and sauté the paste for about 5 minutes, then allow to cool. Add the beef and marinate for at least 3 hours, or ideally overnight. You can make the Chilli-peanut Sauce during marinating time (see page 140).

3 When the beef has marinated sufficiently, thread 4 cubes of beef onto each skewer. Grill over a barbecue or under a hot grill for 1–2 minutes each side, until browned and cooked to your liking. Place 2 skewers on each of 4 plates and serve the Chilli-peanut Sauce separately.

4 Oriental Citrus Kebabs

Prime cut

Preparation and cooking:
30 minutes, plus marinating
and soaking time

Serves 4

½ **tablespoon Szechuan peppercorns, toasted then ground in a coffee-grinder**

½ **tablespoon garlic, mashed to a paste with a little salt**

2 tablespoons fresh ginger, grated

2 tablespoons orange zest, finely grated

4 spring onions (scallions), finely sliced

1 chilli, finely chopped

2 tablespoons runny honey

3 tablespoons soy sauce

150 ml (¼ pint) corn oil

75 ml (2½ fl oz) sesame oil

salt and freshly ground black pepper

700 g (1 lb 9 oz) beef fillet or sirloin, cut into 16 cubes

16 cherry tomatoes

16 fresh bay leaves

16 button mushrooms

The wonderful flavours in these kebabs make them the perfect barbecue food with a twist!

1 In a food processor, blend the ground peppercorns, garlic, ginger, orange zest, spring onions and chilli into a paste.

2 In a large bowl, combine the honey, soy sauce and oils with the paste. Season to taste. Pour over the beef and allow to marinate for at least 4 hours or preferably overnight.

3 Soak 8 bamboo skewers in water for 30 minutes to prevent them from burning. Onto each skewer thread a cherry tomato, followed by a bay leaf, a cube of beef and a button mushroom, and repeat this order once more until the skewers are full. Brush each kebab with the marinade.

4 Cook on a barbecue, under a grill or in a griddle pan for 3–4 minutes each side, or until the beef is cooked to your liking, basting with the marinade juices from time to time. Serve immediately.

Note
Szechuan peppercorns are not usually available in America. Substitute ¾ teaspoon each black peppercorns and aniseed.

5 Bruschetta of Beef Carpaccio, Avocado and Walnuts

Prime cut
Preparation and cooking: 30 minutes, plus freezing time
Serves 4

225 g (8 oz) beef fillet, centre-cut, sinew removed

4 thick slices country bread or focaccia

4 tablespoons extra virgin olive oil

1 clove garlic, peeled

1 handful fresh rocket leaves (arugula), washed and dried

1 avocado, peeled, stoned and sliced lengthways

40 g (1½ oz) (3 tablespoons) Parmesan cheese shavings

2 tablespoons walnuts, chopped

salt and freshly ground black pepper

1 tablespoon walnut oil

juice of 1 lemon

When we discovered Mediterranean cuisine in the early 1990s, bruschetta and crostini were buzz words, bruschetta being the soft country toast and crostini the crisp, brittle bases. This combination works really well as a starter or a light lunch dish. As this dish contains raw beef, it is better to use only the best-quality meat.

1 Wrap the beef in cling film and place in the freezer for about 1½ hours to firm up.

2 Half an hour before serving, sprinkle the bread with half the olive oil and toast it on both sides under the grill or in a ridged griddle pan until golden. Rub the toasted sides with the garlic clove.

3 Remove the beef from the freezer and discard the cling film. Slice the beef very thinly, or gently flatten the slices between sheets of cling film using a rolling pin or meat mallet.

4 Place a few rocket leaves on each bruschetta, top with a couple of thin slices of beef, a couple of slices of avocado, some Parmesan shavings and a scattering of walnuts. Season to taste.

5 Combine the remaining olive oil, walnut oil and lemon juice and sprinkle over the bruschetta.

Variation
Omit the avocado and walnuts in step 4.

6 Brochette of Beef Fillet with Anchovy

Prime cut
Preparation and cooking: 30 minutes, plus soaking time
Serves 4

100 ml (3¹/₂ fl oz) extra virgin olive oil

2 cloves garlic, crushed to a paste with a little salt

12 anchovy fillets, 4 of which are cut in half

450 g (1 lb) beef fillet, cut into 16 x 2.5 cm (1 inch) cubes

4 rashers (slices) smoked streaky bacon, each cut into 3 pieces

8 cherry tomatoes

8 button mushrooms

For those of you who have seen me on TV, you will know I am a big fan of anchovies. They go well with many meats, but especially with this perfect barbecue number.

1 Soak 4 long bamboo skewers in cold water for 30 minutes to prevent them from burning.

2 Heat the olive oil in a pan over a low heat. Add the garlic and the 8 whole anchovy fillets. Cook until the anchovies melt or break down; help them along by mashing them with a fork. Set aside to cool.

3 Thread a cube of beef onto a skewer, followed by a piece of bacon, a piece of anchovy, a tomato, a mushroom, then beef, tomato, bacon, anchovy, beef, mushroom, bacon and finishing with a cube of beef. Repeat with the remaining skewers.

4 Baste the brochettes with the anchovy oil. Place them on a hot barbecue, under a hot grill or in a hot griddle pan and cook for about 1–2 minutes on each of the four sides, basting occasionally with anchovy oil. Serve with a green salad.

7 Beef Consommé 'Tea'

Good-value cut
Preparation and cooking: 1 hour
Serves 4

225 g (8 oz) lean beef from the shin (shank), flank or skirt

1 celery stalk, finely diced

1 small carrot, finely diced

I remember my gran used to have hot Bovril before she went to bed. This beautifully clear soup is a far nicer substitute. It requires a little effort but has a beautiful flavour and is very healthy.

1 Trim the beef of all fat, then mince (grind) or finely chop the meat. In a bowl, mix the meat with the vegetables, parsley and egg whites. Put the stock and red wine into a saucepan and stir in the meat and vegetable mixture. Bring slowly to the boil, stirring continuously, ensuring that none of the mixture sticks to the pan.

(continued opposite)

1 small onion, finely chopped

1 leek, cut into 5 mm (¼ inch) dice

1 tablespoon fresh parsley, finely chopped

2 egg whites, lightly beaten

1.2 litres (2 pints) beef stock

300 ml (½ pint) red wine

salt and freshly ground black pepper

2 Reduce the heat and simmer gently for 40 minutes without stirring. By this time the egg white will have coagulated into a crust which will act as a filter for the consommé. Place a piece of muslin over a colander and place the colander over a bowl. Carefully strain the contents of the pan through the muslin and colander, into the bowl. Discard the solids.

3 Season the consommé and serve, or allow to cool and refrigerate until required.

8 Beef Carpaccio with Balsamic Vinegar

Prime cut
Preparation and cooking: 20 minutes
Makes 18 crostini

18 slices French bread (baguette), 5 mm (¼ inch) thick

6 tablespoons virgin olive oil

1 handful fresh rocket leaves (arugula)

2 tablespoons reduced balsamic vinegar (see Tip below)

salt and ground black pepper

175 g (6 oz) beef fillet, sliced paper-thin

50 g (2 oz) (¼ cup) Parmesan cheese shavings

1 tablespoon fresh chives, snipped

1 tablespoon lemon zest

Having suffered during the BSE and foot-and-mouth scares, raw beef is back on the menu with a vengeance now. This is a lovely open sandwich that will particularly appeal if you are a big raw-beef fan. Make sure you use top-quality meat as in this recipe it is not cooked.

1 Preheat the oven to 180°C/350°F/Gas Mark 4. Spread out the bread slices on a large baking sheet and toast in the oven for about 15 minutes, until crisp and slightly golden. Allow the crostini to cool.

2 Brush each crostini with olive oil and place a little rocket on top.

3 For the dressing, combine the reduced vinegar, the remaining oil, and salt and pepper to taste. Dip the beef slices quickly in the dressing and place on top of each rocket crostini. To serve, garnish with the Parmesan shavings, chives and lemon zest, season and arrange on a platter.

Tip
To reduce the balsamic vinegar, pour into a saucepan and simmer over a medium heat until reduced by one-third. Allow to cool, then rebottle.

9 Sukiyaki Beef Rolls

Prime cut
Preparation and cooking: 30 minutes, plus marinating time
Serves 4

450 g (1 lb) beef fillet, sliced 3 mm (¹⁄₈ inch) thick across the grain (about 16 slices)

About 1 tablespoon wasabi Japanese horseradish

2 sheets nori (dried seaweed), 20 x 19 cm (8 x 7½ inch), cut into 16 strips of 10 x 4.5 cm (4 x 1¾ inch)

4 spring onions (scallions), each cut on the diagonal into thin slices

8 shiitake mushrooms, stalks removed, sliced into thin strips

cornflour (cornstarch), for rolling

COOKING SAUCE

300 ml (½ pint) water

2 teaspoons dashi stock powder

3 tablespoons soy sauce

1 bunch spring onions (scallions), white parts only, cut into 10 cm (4 inch) slivers

2 tablespoons sugar

25 g (1 oz) (¼ cup) cornflour (cornstarch)

4 tablespoons vegetable oil

1 beaten egg per person

MARINADE

see method for ingredients

Japanese food is becoming increasingly popular as it is perceived to be very healthy and the presentation is always excellent. This is my variation on a classic. If desired, you can serve this the traditional way – with a beaten egg in a sauce bowl for each person in which to dip their beef rolls.

1 For the marinade, mix together all the ingredients (see below). Add the beef slices and marinate for 1 hour.

2 Remove a slice of beef from the marinade and shake off the excess liquid. Place on a flat surface and carefully spread a little wasabi over the slice. Place 1 nori strip on top of the wasabi. Place 2 or 3 slivers of spring onion and shiitake mushrooms at one end of the beef slice. Starting at the end with the onion and mushrooms, roll up the beef slice and secure it with a wooden cocktail stick. Roll in the cornflour and place on a platter. Repeat to make the rest of the beef rolls. Reserve the remaining marinade.

3 For the cooking sauce, combine the water, dashi stock powder, soy sauce, spring onions, sugar and cornflour with the reserved marinade. In a large frying pan, heat the oil over a high heat. Add the beef rolls and pan-fry on all sides for 2–3 minutes. Reduce the heat then pour in the sauce mixture. Simmer the rolls for 8–10 minutes until the sauce becomes glazed.

4 Remove the cocktail sticks from the rolls. Cut the rolls in half and serve warm. If desired, serve a beaten egg in a sauce bowl for each person and invite guests to dip each bite into the beaten egg.

Marinade ingredients
175 ml (6 fl oz) soy sauce, ½ teaspoon grated fresh ginger, 6 tablespoons mirin and ½ teaspoon wasabi Japanese horseradish.

10 Beef Fillet Tonnato

Prime cut
Preparation and cooking: 30 minutes over two days
Serves 6–8

1 tablespoon olive oil

900 g (2 lb) fillet of beef, centre-cut

2 glasses red wine

1 medium onion, peeled and halved

1 celery stalk

1 carrot, peeled

1 bay leaf

2 cloves

salt and freshly ground black pepper

1 small can of tuna fish in oil, drained

2 anchovies

1 raw egg yolk

2 hard-boiled (hard-cooked) egg yolks

150 ml (¼ pint) olive oil

1 tablespoon lemon juice, plus lemon slices

2 tablespoons gherkins, chopped

1 teaspoon capers

cayenne pepper, for dusting

This stems from a classic Italian veal dish, but try this and you won't go looking for veal ever again.

1 Heat the oil in a large frying pan over a medium heat, then brown the beef fillet all over. Place the beef in a saucepan just large enough to take the fillet. Pour enough boiling water into the pan to cover the beef and add the wine, onion, celery stalk, carrot, bay leaf, cloves and seasoning. Bring back to the boil. Turn off the heat as soon as it reaches boiling point and allow the fillet to cool in the liquor overnight.

2 Blend the tuna fish with the anchovies, raw egg yolk and the hard-boiled egg yolks in a food processor. With the machine running, drizzle the olive oil into the sauce and blend until emulsified. If too thick, add a little beef cooking liquor, then season to taste with salt, pepper and lemon juice. The consistency should be creamy enough to coat a spoon.

3 Slice the beef very thinly, arrange on a serving dish, cover with the sauce and decorate with chopped gherkins, capers and thin lemon slices, and dust with cayenne pepper.

11 Steak Tartare with Butter-fried Oysters

Prime cut
Preparation and cooking: 30 minutes
Serves 2

280 g (10 oz) beef sirloin, trimmed of fat and finely ground

1 tablespoon spring onion (scallion), finely chopped

1 tablespoon fresh flat-leaf parsley, finely chopped

2 teaspoons Dijon mustard

2 teaspoons gherkins, chopped

1 teaspoon capers, chopped

2 anchovies, chopped

1 teaspoon red chilli, finely diced, or Tabasco sauce

1 teaspoon Worcestershire sauce

1 raw egg yolk

$\frac{1}{2}$ teaspoon salt

1 teaspoon freshly ground black pepper

50 g (2 oz) ($\frac{1}{4}$ cup) unsalted butter

12 shucked oysters (keep the shells)

There is a classic joke about a customer who asked for steak tartare well-done. It is of course a raw dish, and despite my wife's preference for well-done meat, I have persuaded her to enjoy this dish. Buy some top-quality beef, give it a try and you will surprise yourself.

1 Put the beef, spring onion, parsley, mustard, gherkins, capers, anchovies, chilli or Tabasco, Worcestershire sauce, egg yolk, salt and pepper into a bowl, and blend with a fork until just mixed. Form the mixture into two burgers and refrigerate until ready to eat.

2 Heat half the butter in a frying pan until foaming. Dry the oysters and add them to the frying pan six at a time. Cook over a fierce heat until the edges curl, turning once. Remove from the pan, then repeat with the second six, adding extra butter as necessary. Season to taste.

3 Place the oysters in their own shells and circle them around the tartare. Serve with hot buttered toast.

12 Terrine of Oxtail and Winter Vegetables with Sauce Gribiche

Good-value cut
Preparation and cooking: 4 hours 30 minutes over 3 days
Serves 10–12

PREPARATION

2 kg (4 lb 8 oz) oxtail, cut into 5cm (2 inch) pieces

2 whole carrots, peeled

2 whole leeks, washed

2 onions, peeled

2 celery stalks

1 teaspoon black peppercorns

1 bouquet garni (see method for ingredients)

600 ml (1 pint) beef stock

600 ml (1 pint) red wine

salt

TERRINE

2 tablespoons fresh parsley, chopped

1½ tablespoons baby capers, rinsed

2 gherkins, cut into very small dice

1 tablespoon green pepper-corns, drained

salt and freshly ground black pepper

8 baby carrots, scraped

6 baby leeks, washed

4 celery stalks

6 quail eggs, hard-boiled (hard-cooked) and peeled

Cooked oxtail produces a wonderfully gelatinous stock which binds this fabulous terrine together. Definitely one for the dinner party repertoire.

1 Two days before you plan to serve the terrine, place the oxtail in a large saucepan and cover with water. Bring to the boil, then reduce the heat and simmer for 30 minutes. Drain and discard the water; this gets rid of any impurities.

2 Return the oxtail to a clean saucepan, add all the preparation ingredients and cover with water. Bring to the boil, then reduce the heat and simmer gently, covered, for approximately 3 hours. Skim the liquid of any scum that appears on the surface, and top up with water as necessary to keep the oxtail covered. Allow to cool, then refrigerate overnight.

3 The next day, remove any fat that has solidified on the surface. Warm the oxtail gently to melt the jellied liquid, then remove the oxtail to a chopping board and trim and discard any fat. Shred the oxtail meat with two forks and set aside in a bowl, discarding the bones. Discard the remaining vegetables.

4 Place the cooking liquid on the stove and bring to the boil. Cook until the liquid has reduced to about 425 ml (¾ pint), skimming from time to time. Allow to cool, then combine with the meat from the oxtail.

5 For the terrine, add the parsley, capers, gherkins and green peppercorns to the oxtail and toss to combine. Check the seasoning, remembering the terrine will be eaten cold; you might want to boost the seasoning a bit.

6 Cook the carrots, leeks and celery stalks until tender. Place a 1 cm (½ inch) layer of oxtail in the bottom of an oiled terrine, then place a row of the cooked carrots, leeks and celery lengthways on top of the oxtail. Place another layer of oxtail on top, pushing down, then place a row of quail eggs down the centre, and top with oxtail. Repeat, using up the vegetables and oxtail, finishing with a layer of oxtail. Cover with foil and place a weight on top to compress the mixture. Refrigerate overnight.

(continued opposite)

SAUCE GRIBICHE

2 shallots, finely chopped

3 tablespoons fresh parsley, finely chopped

2 tablespoons fresh chives, snipped

$\frac{1}{2}$ tablespoon fresh tarragon leaves, finely chopped

juice and grated zest of 1 unwaxed lemon

2 tablespoons capers, chopped

3 baby gherkins, finely chopped

$\frac{1}{2}$ teaspoon ground white pepper

2 hard-boiled (hard-cooked) eggs, peeled and chopped

300 ml ($\frac{1}{2}$ pint) good mayonnaise

300 ml ($\frac{1}{2}$ pint) crème fraîche (sour cream)

3 tomatoes, deseeded and cut into 5 mm ($\frac{1}{4}$ inch) dice

7 For the sauce gribiche, combine the shallots, parsley, chives, tarragon, lemon juice and zest, capers, baby gherkins, pepper and eggs and set aside. Beat together the mayonnaise and crème fraîche. Fold the herb mixture into the mayonnaise mixture and season to taste. Fold in the tomatoes just before serving.

8 Cut the terrine into slices and serve with the sauce gribiche and grilled country bread.

To make a home-made bouquet garni

Take 2 sticks celery, 2 strips leek, 2 sprigs fresh thyme, 4 fresh parsley stalks and 2 fresh bay leaves and tie into a neat bundle with string. Alternatively, you can buy a packet of bouquet garni from your supermarket.

13 Mini Yorkshire Puds with Roast Beef and Horseradish Cream

Prime cut
Preparation and cooking: 1 hour
Makes 12 Yorkshire puddings

1 clove garlic

3 anchovies

2 eggs

75 ml (2½ fl oz) milk

75 ml (2½ fl oz) water

salt and freshly ground black pepper

100 g (4 oz) (¼ cup) plain flour (all-purpose flour), sifted

a little vegetable oil

12 thin slices rare roast beef

2 tablespoons Horseradish Cream (for ingredients and method see page 130)

Do you remember the days when canapés used to consist of rubbery toast and a scant topping coated with a thick layer of aspic jelly? Thank God those days have gone, to be replaced by more substantial mini dishes in a mouthful.

1 Preheat the oven to 200°C/400°F/Gas Mark 6. In a pestle and mortar, crush the garlic clove together with the anchovies. Beat together the eggs, milk, water, garlic-anchovy paste and seasoning in a bowl, then whisk in the flour. Leave to rest for 30 minutes then pass through a sieve. It should be the consistency of single cream (half-and-half cream), so if the mixture is too thick, add a little more water.

2 Lightly grease 12 moulds of a mini-muffin tray with the oil. Heat the tray until very hot, then divide the batter between the 12 moulds. Cook for about 15 minutes, until risen and fluffy.

3 Spread the slices of beef thinly with the Horseradish Cream. Roll up and pop into the Yorkshire puddings. Season with black pepper and serve immediately.

14 French Beef Salad

Prime cut
Preparation and cooking: 40 minutes, plus resting time
Serves 6

750 g (1 lb 10 oz) waxy new potatoes, unpeeled

500–750 g (1 lb 2 oz–1 lb 10 oz) rare roast beef, cut into 1 cm (½ inch) slices

3 hard-boiled (hard-cooked) eggs, quartered

3 medium tomatoes, peeled and quartered

DRESSING

1 teaspoon Dijon mustard, or to taste

3 tablespoons aged red wine vinegar

1 teaspoon runny honey

salt and freshly ground black pepper

9 tablespoons olive oil

2 shallots, very finely chopped

2 tablespoons fresh chives, snipped

2 tablespoons fresh parsley, very finely chopped

1½ tablespoons capers, very finely chopped

1½ tablespoons gherkins, very finely chopped

1 clove garlic, crushed with a little salt (optional)

A classic salad with lovely new potatoes, and a great way of using up your Sunday roast. The capers, gherkins and herbs create wonderful flavours and textures.

1 Put the potatoes in cold salted water, cover and bring to the boil. Simmer for 15–20 minutes, or until just tender, then drain. Cut the beef slices into thin strips.

2 For the dressing, whisk the mustard with the vinegar, honey and seasoning, then gradually beat in the oil so the dressing emulsifies. Stir in the shallots, chives, parsley, capers, gherkins and garlic, if using.

3 While the potatoes are still warm, cut them into 1 cm (½ inch) slices and arrange some of the slices in a layer in the bottom of a salad bowl. Spoon a little dressing over the potatoes, then cover with a layer of beef and a spoonful of dressing. Repeat the layers, spooning a little dressing over each one, and ending with a layer of potatoes. Cover and leave the salad in a cool place, or in the refrigerator, for at least 2 hours, but ideally up to 12 hours, for the flavours to mingle.

4 A short time before serving, alternate the eggs and tomatoes around the edge of the salad.

15 Chargrilled Thai Beef Salad

Prime cut
Preparation and cooking: 40 minutes, plus marinating time
Serves 4

1 tablespoon jasmine rice, uncooked

2 dried red chillies

500 g (1 lb 2 oz) thick fillet steak

2 tablespoons sesame oil

75 ml (2½ fl oz) *kecap manis* (sweet soy sauce)

2 teaspoons sugar

4 tablespoons lime juice

3 tablespoons Thai fish sauce (*nam pla*)

1 small cucumber, peeled, deseeded, halved lengthways and cut into 1 cm (½ inch) slices

4 red shallots, finely sliced

12 cherry tomatoes, halved

2 red chillies, finely sliced

1 handful fresh mint leaves

1 handful fresh coriander leaves (cilantro)

2 tablespoons fresh basil leaves, ripped

4 spring onions (scallions), finely sliced

On my various trips to Thailand I have been impressed by the imaginative salads. This one is no exception. It has wonderful fresh flavours, and is perfect if you are on one of those perpetual diets.

1 Heat a dry frying pan, add the rice and toast until golden but not burnt. Grind the rice in a clean coffee-grinder or pound to a powder and set aside. Reheat the frying pan and add the dried red chillies. Toast until they are smoky, then grind or pound to a powder and set aside.

2 Chargrill or pan-fry the beef for around 12 minutes, until well-marked outside and rare to medium-rare inside. Place in a bowl and leave to rest for 10 minutes. Meanwhile, combine the sesame oil with the *kecap manis* and brush over the fillet. Marinate for 2 hours.

3 Dissolve the sugar in the lime juice and fish sauce. Combine half a teaspoon of the ground dried chilli powder with half a teaspoon of the ground rice and set aside. Combine the cucumber, shallots, cherry tomatoes, red chillies, herbs and spring onions in a large bowl. Add the lime juice and fish sauce mixture and toss to combine.

4 Slice the beef thinly. Toss the beef and ground rice mix through the salad along with any cooking juices that have collected in the beef bowl. Pile high on a large platter and serve with a salad of crunchy raw lettuce.

16 Seared Beef Carpaccio with Avocado and Beetroot Salad

Prime cut
Preparation time: 1 hour 20 minutes
Serves 6

6 medium red beetroot (beets), trimmed and washed

2 tablespoons red wine vinegar

200 ml (7 fl oz) extra virgin olive oil, plus extra for brushing

Maldon salt (sea salt) and freshly ground pepper

1 kg (2 lb 4 oz) beef fillet, centre-cut

1 tablespoon Dijon mustard

2 tablespoons coriander seeds, crushed

2 firm, ripe avocados

sprigs of fresh chervil

CITRUS DRESSING

1 large shallot, finely chopped

2 tablespoons white wine vinegar

2 tablespoons lemon juice

2 tablespoons orange juice

$1/2$ teaspoon lemon zest

$1/2$ teaspoon orange zest

2 tablespoons fresh chervil, chopped

I discovered a similar recipe to this in Alice Walters' Chez Panise restaurant in Berkeley, California – a wonderful restaurant and a wonderful combination of flavours. For a variation, try avocado on its own with citrus dressing.

1 Preheat the oven to 200°C/400°F/Gas Mark 6.

2 Place the beetroot in a roasting tray. Add a splash of water to the tray and cover tightly with foil. Place the beetroot in the oven and roast for 1 hour, or until tender. Remove from the oven, uncover the tray, and leave the beetroot until cool enough to handle. Peel the beetroot and cut each into 6 wedges. Place in a bowl and add the red wine vinegar and 1 tablespoon of the olive oil and season generously.

3 Lightly paint the beef fillet with the mustard. Sprinkle a board or large, flat plate with the coriander seeds and 1 teaspoon each of salt and freshly ground black pepper. Roll the beef in the seasoning to encrust it.

4 Heat a griddle pan until very hot and lightly brush it with oil. Add the beef and sear for about 6 minutes, turning regularly until browned all over. Remove from the pan and allow to rest. The beef will be blue in the centre; if you prefer it more well-done, adjust the cooking time accordingly.

5 For the dressing, place the chopped shallot in a bowl and add the white wine vinegar, lemon juice, orange juice and a pinch of salt. Whisk in the remaining olive oil and stir in the lemon and orange zest with the chopped chervil. Season to taste.

6 Cut the avocados in half lengthways and remove the stones and skin. Cut lengthways into 5 mm ($1/4$ inch) slices. Slice the beef as thinly as you can. Arrange the avocado slices and beetroot wedges alternately on a platter. Drizzle with citrus dressing and top with the slices of beef and sprigs of chervil.

17 Cold Beef Fillet with Tomato and Herb Dressing

Prime cut
Preparation and cooking: 1 hour 30 minutes, plus refrigeration time
Serves 4

450 g (1 lb) beef fillet, centre-cut

2 tablespoons extra virgin olive oil

1 tablespoon coarsely ground black peppercorns

100 ml (3½ fl oz) dry martini

TOMATO AND HERB DRESSING

1 tablespoon freshly squeezed lemon juice

4 plum tomatoes, peeled, deseeded and diced

1 tablespoon each fresh tarragon, chervil, parsley and basil, roughly chopped

1 tablespoon coarsely ground coriander

4 tablespoons extra virgin olive oil

salt and freshly ground pepper

WATERCRESS SALAD

2 bunches watercress, tough stems removed

1 tablespoon fresh chervil, chopped

10 tablespoons extra virgin olive oil

3 tablespoons red wine vinegar

salt and freshly ground pepper

I love beef salads, especially when they are made with fillet because you can roast it in advance until rare, and it then cuts nice and thinly and becomes a very economical dish.

1 Preheat the oven to 220°C/425°F/Gas Mark 7. Remove the beef from the refrigerator at least half an hour before cooking to bring it to room temperature. Pat the surface with a paper towel. Rub with the olive oil and coarsely ground peppercorns, pressing them firmly into the meat.

2 Place the meat in a large roasting pan and pop it into the oven for 10 minutes, turning once so all the sides are seared, then lower the heat to 160°C/325°F/Gas Mark 3 and cook for a further 15 minutes.

3 Remove the beef from the oven and cool to room temperature. Meanwhile, add a little martini to the roasting pan and scrape the coagulated juices from the bottom of the pan. Pour the juices into a large bowl with the beef, cover with cling film and refrigerate.

4 A few hours before you are ready to serve, remove the meat and juices from the refrigerator. Discard any solidified fat from the juices. Place the meat on a board and cut crossways into slices about 1 cm (½ inch) thick. Carefully spoon the meat juices onto each slice of beef. Replace the slices tightly against each other, wrap them in cling film and set aside until ready to use.

5 Meanwhile, prepare the tomato and herb dressing. Place the lemon juice and tomatoes in a bowl with the herbs. Add the ground coriander, olive oil and seasoning, and stir. Cover and leave until ready to serve.

6 For the watercress salad, combine the watercress with the chervil, then toss with the olive oil, vinegar and seasoning.

7 Arrange the beef slices on a platter or individual plates, dribble with any meat juices, followed by the tomato and herb dressing. Serve the watercress salad on the side.

18 Asian Beef Sandwich with Black Bean & Garlic Mayonnaise

Good-value cut
Preparation and cooking: 30 minutes, plus marinating time
Makes 8 sandwiches

125 ml (4 fl oz) each ground-nut (peanut) oil, soy sauce and rice wine or dry sherry

1 tablespoon toasted sesame oil

2 tablespoons garlic, finely chopped

4 spring onions (scallions), sliced 2.5 cm (1 inch) thick on the angle

½ tablespoon coarsely ground black pepper

1 kg (2 lb 4 oz) rump, sirloin or fillet steak, sliced 1 cm (½ inch) thick, and each slice cut into 1 cm (½ inch) pieces

2 tablespoons canola oil

1 large red onion, cut into 5 mm (¼ inch) slices

2 hot chillies, finely chopped with seeds removed

half a head of Chinese leaves (Chinese cabbage) or pak choi, cut into 5 mm (¼ inch) slices

1 each red and green pepper (bell pepper), cored, deseeded and julienned

1 carrot, cut into matchsticks

1 handful (mung) beansprouts

8 pitta (pita) breads

BLACK BEAN & GARLIC MAYONNAISE

see method for ingredients

I love my sarnies, but tend to get bored with run-of-the-mill offerings in sandwich bars and supermarkets. Give this one a try; it looks like there are a lot of ingredients but it's well worth the effort.

1 In a medium-sized bowl, combine the groundnut oil, soy sauce, rice wine, sesame oil, garlic, spring onion and pepper. Add the beef, stir to coat, cover and marinate in the refrigerator for at least 4 hours and preferably overnight, turning from time to time.

2 Preheat the oven to 140°C/275°F/Gas Mark 1. Heat a wok over a high heat. Add the canola oil and swirl to coat the pan. When the oil is very hot, add the red onions and chillies and stir-fry for around 3 minutes, until tender-crisp. Add the beef and stir-fry for around 3 minutes, until the meat is seared on the outside and rare within; do not overcook. Remove and set aside. Add the Chinese leaves, red and green peppers, carrots, beansprouts and any remaining marinade and stir-fry for around 4 minutes, until tender-crisp, then return the beef mix to the pan.

3 Meanwhile, warm the pitta breads in the oven. Cut a pocket through one side of each pitta and spread the insides with the mayonnaise (see below). Stuff generously with the beef mixture and serve.

To make the Black Bean & Garlic Mayonnaise

Heat a frying pan over a medium heat. Add 2 tablespoons groundnut (peanut) oil and swirl to coat the pan. When the oil is hot, add 3 tablespoons finely chopped garlic, 1 tablespoon fermented Chinese black beans (that have been rinsed and finely chopped) and 1 tablespoon finely chopped fresh ginger. Fry the ingredients, stirring, for 3 to 5 minutes or until soft. Then add 2 tablespoons rice wine vinegar and cook for about 3 minutes or until reduced by three-quarters. Allow to cool completely.

In a food processor, combine the vinegar mixture with 2 raw egg yolks and blend. With the machine running, slowly drizzle 1 pint of groundnut oil through the feed tube. When the mixture emulsifies, add the oil more quickly until the mixture is mayonnaise-like. Season with salt and pepper to taste. If not using immediately, store covered in the refrigerator.

19 Alternative Open Steak Sandwich

Prime cut
Preparation and cooking: 30 minutes
Makes 2 sandwiches

50 g (2 oz) (¼ cup) beef dripping (fat from roasted meat)

85 g (3 oz) smoked streaky bacon, cut into lardons (or 3–4 slices, cut into small strips)

3 spring onions (scallions), finely sliced

4 precooked new potatoes, thinly sliced

1 head chicory (Belgian endive), thinly shredded

2 tablespoons fresh parsley, chopped

salt and freshly ground black pepper

280 g (10 oz) beef fillet, cut into 6 thin slices

2 tablespoons beef stock

2 tablespoons red wine

1 tablespoon diced bone marrow (optional)

1 tablespoon Parmesan cheese, freshly grated

2 thick slices toasted country bread

This is a fabulous sandwich with a whole host of wonderful flavours, using traditional ingredients such as chicory and bone marrow. Definitely a meal in itself.

1 Heat half the beef dripping in a pan over a medium heat, then add the bacon, spring onions, new potatoes and chicory and pan-fry until the bacon is cooked and the vegetables are golden. Fold in the parsley, season to taste, then set aside to keep warm.

2 In a separate large frying pan, melt the remaining dripping over a high heat. Season the slices of beef, then cook them for 1½ minutes each side for medium-rare, or to your liking. Remove from the pan and rest in a warm place for 1 minute.

3 Over a high heat, pour the beef stock into the beef pan, followed by the red wine, bone marrow, if using, and the Parmesan. Swirl to combine, adding any juices that may have leaked from the resting beef.

4 Top each slice of toast with the bacon and vegetable mixture. Top each pile with three slices of beef, dribble over the cheesy meat juices and serve immediately.

20 Salt-Beef Sandwich

Good-value cut
Preparation and cooking: 4 hours 10 minutes
Makes 4 sandwiches

2 kg (4 lb 8 oz) salt beef, ready-soaked

2 onions, peeled

2 carrots, peeled

2 celery stalks

4 bay leaves

½ tablespoon black peppercorns

10 juniper berries

8 slices rye bread

butter, for spreading

horseradish sauce, for spreading

Dijon mustard, for spreading

Jewish pickled cucumbers (Kosher dill pickles), to serve

If you've ever been to a Jewish deli in New York and attempted to get your mouth round a salt-beef sandwich, you'll know it's almost impossible as the sandwiches are about five inches thick. Obviously you can make thinner ones, but whatever you do is bound to be popular.

1 Place the beef in a large saucepan and cover with plenty of water. Bring to the boil, then reduce the heat and simmer for 1 hour, removing any scum that floats to the surface.

2 Add the onion, carrot, celery, bay leaves, peppercorns and juniper berries and continue to simmer for a further 3 hours, or until you can pierce the meat easily with a fork.

3 For a classic New York salt-beef sandwich, butter the slices of rye bread, then spread 4 slices with horseradish sauce and the other 4 with Dijon mustard. Place 7.5–10 cm (3–4 inches) of finely shaved hot beef onto the slices of bread spread with horseradish. Top with the mustard-spread slices and serve with pickled cucumbers.

21 A Retrospective Steak Sandwich

Prime cut
Preparation and cooking: 1 hour, plus marinating time
Makes 2 sandwiches

2 tablespoons balsamic vinegar

1 clove garlic, finely chopped

1 small dried chilli, crushed

1 teaspoon fresh oregano, chopped

2 x 115–140 g (4–5 oz) sirloin steaks, 1 cm (½ inch) thick

25 g (1 oz) (2 tablespoons) unsalted butter, plus 50 g (2 oz) (¼ cup), softened

2 leeks, washed and thinly sliced

2 tablespoons muscovado (dark brown) sugar

2 tablespoons dry white wine

4 thick slices sourdough bread

salt and ground black pepper

2 large handfuls fresh wild rocket (arugula)

50 g (2 oz) (½ cup) Roquefort

WARM TOMATO SALSA

2 tablespoons olive oil

1 red onion, finely sliced

1 clove garlic, chopped

1 small dried chilli

350 g (12 oz) baby plum tomatoes

1 tablespoon balsamic vinegar

1 tablespoon fresh oregano, finely chopped

Who doesn't like a steak sandwich? Here I provide you with a little cheffy interpretation involving cooked tomatoes and caramelized leeks – it's well worth trying.

1 Mix together the balsamic vinegar, garlic, chilli and oregano in a shallow dish. Add the steaks and leave to marinate for 2 hours.

2 Fifteen minutes before cooking the steaks, make the salsa. Gently heat the olive oil in a frying pan. Add the onion, garlic and chilli and gently cook for 5–10 minutes until the onion is soft and golden. Add the tomatoes and cook for 3–4 minutes until the tomatoes begin to soften. Stir in the balsamic vinegar and oregano and cook for a further minute. Season to taste.

3 Melt the 25 g (2 tablespoons) butter over a medium heat in a frying pan, add the leeks and cook for 8–10 minutes until wilted. Add the sugar and dry white wine and cook gently for 20 minutes until the leeks have caramelized.

4 Meanwhile, spread the 50 g (¼ cup) softened butter on one side of each piece of bread and season. Grill the buttered side of the bread for 1–2 minutes and set aside. Place the rocket in a bowl and roughly crumble in the Roquefort cheese.

5 Remove the steaks from the marinade and season with salt and pepper. Sear on a barbecue or griddle pan for 1 minute each side; reduce the cooking time if you like your steaks rare.

6 To assemble the sandwiches, divide the rocket and Roquefort salad between two pieces of the toasted bread and top each with a steak. Spoon over the warm tomato salsa and top each with caramelized leeks and the remaining slices of grilled bread. Cut each sandwich in half on the diagonal and serve immediately.

22 Caesar Steak Sandwich

Prime cut
Preparation and cooking: 20 minutes
Makes 2 sandwiches

2 x 140 g (5 oz) fat-free sirloin steaks

salt and ground black pepper

1 tablespoon olive oil

1 Little Gem lettuce (crunchy lettuce, such as romaine)

15 g (½ oz) (1 tablespoon) Parmesan cheese, freshly grated

2 large pitta (pita) breads

4 anchovy fillets (optional)

CAESAR SALAD DRESSING

2 egg yolks

1 tablespoon red wine vinegar

1 tablespoon freshly squeezed lemon juice

5 anchovy fillets, mashed to a paste

1 teaspoon anchovy essence (extract)

3 cloves garlic, mashed to a paste

1 tablespoon Dijon mustard

1 teaspoon Colman's English mustard powder

½ tablespoon freshly ground black pepper

2 teaspoons Worcestershire sauce

300 ml (½ pint) good olive oil

Caesar salad has to be one of the all-time favourites for ladies who lunch. Surprisingly, the addition of beef makes an excellent sandwich. No diet food here!

1 For the caesar salad dressing, blend together all the ingredients except the oil in a food processor. I like my dressing quite peppery, so reduce the quantity of pepper if this is not to your liking. With the machine running, add the oil in a slow trickle. Refrigerate the dressing until required.

2 Beat the steaks with a meat mallet or rolling pin until slightly thinner. Season them with salt and freshly ground black pepper.

3 Heat a heavy-based frying pan, add the olive oil and cook the steaks over a fierce heat for 1 minute each side. Cut the steaks into strips and keep warm.

4 Meanwhile, shred the lettuce thinly and combine with a little dressing to coat. The remainder of the dressing can be kept in the fridge for up to a week. Toss the coated lettuce with the Parmesan cheese.

5 Toast the pitta breads, then cut a large pocket in them, leaving them 'hinged' by not cutting them all the way through. Divide the salad evenly between the two pitta breads, then top with the steaks and the anchovy fillets (each cut lengthways in two), if using. Drizzle a little more dressing over the steaks. Fold over the pitta flaps and eat immediately.

23 Steak and Eggs

Prime cut
Preparation and cooking: 30 minutes
Serves 4

1 tablespoon Worcestershire sauce

juice of ½ lemon

4 x 200 g (7 oz) fat-free sirloin steaks

8 large free-range eggs

2 teaspoons Horseradish Cream (see page 130)

1 tablespoon fresh chives, snipped

salt and freshly ground black pepper

1 tablespoon olive oil

50 g (2 oz) (¼ cup) unsalted butter

2 tablespoons double cream (heavy cream)

A bit of a cliché in America but a really lovely brunch dish all the same.

1 Combine the Worcestershire sauce with the lemon juice and brush both sides of the steaks with the mixture. Set the steaks aside at room temperature for 30 minutes to flavour.

2 Break the eggs into a bowl and beat together with the Horseradish Cream and chives until just combined; do not overbeat. Season with salt and pepper

3 Heat the olive oil in a griddle pan or large frying pan. Season the steaks with salt and pepper and cook them over a high heat for 2 minutes each side for medium-rare, or to your liking. Remove the steaks from the pan and set aside to rest in a warm place for 3 minutes.

4 Heat a non-stick saucepan or large frying pan, add the butter and cook until foaming but not brown. Add the cream, bring to the boil, then pour in the eggs. Stir the eggs with a wooden spoon, drawing them into the centre to create a curd effect. When scrambled to your liking, remove from the heat and divide between 4 warm plates. Place a steak next to the eggs on each plate and serve immediately.

24 Cornish Pasty

Good-value cut

Preparation and cooking:
1 hour 10 minutes

Makes 2 very large pasties or
4 modest ones

450 g (1 lb) shortcrust pastry
(ideally made with lard)

450 g (1 lb) chuck steak

140 g (5 oz) (1¾ cups) onion,
finely diced

100 g (4 oz) (1½ cups) swede
(rutabaga), peeled and thinly
sliced

175 g (6 oz) (2 cups) potato,
peeled and thinly sliced

½ teaspoon fresh soft thyme
leaves

pinch cayenne pepper

½ teaspoon freshly ground
black pepper

¼ teaspoon salt

1 egg, beaten

The Cornish got very upset when I cooked this dish on *Food and Drink* because I pre-fried my beef and used Worcestershire sauce – oops! I have since modified the recipe to appease them, although I have simplified the pastry.

1 Preheat the oven to 200°C/400°F/Gas Mark 6. Roll out the pastry and cut out two circles the size of dinner plates, about 23 cm (9 inches) in diameter.

2 Trim the meat of any sinew, gristle or fat. Cut the meat into 5 mm (¼ inch) dice and combine with the onion, swede, potato, thyme, peppers and salt. Arrange the meat mixture down the middle of each circle of pastry, leaving 2.5 cm (1 inch) at each end. Brush the edges of the circles with a little of the beaten egg.

3 Either bring the two edges together over the meat or fold one side over to meet the other. Pinch or crimp the pastry together to make a tight seal and place on a baking sheet. Brush with the beaten egg. Cook the pasties for 20–25 minutes, then reduce the heat to 160°C/325°F/Gas Mark 3 and cook for a further 40 minutes. Serve hot or cold.

25 Fillet of Beef with Two Sauces

Prime cut
Preparation and cooking: 40 minutes
Serves 4

1 tablespoon olive oil

50 g (2 oz) (¼ cup) unsalted butter

4 x 175 g (6 oz) beef fillet steaks, centre-cut

Maldon salt (sea salt) and freshly ground black pepper

100 ml (3½ fl oz) dry white wine

6 tablespoons beef stock

BEURRE BERCY

140 g (5 oz) (½ cup plus 2 tablespoons) unsalted butter

3 shallots, finely chopped

100 ml (3½ fl oz) dry white wine

225 g (8 oz) bone marrow (optional), poached for a few minutes in nearly boiling salted water and then well drained

1 tablespoon fresh parsley, chopped

2 teaspoons lemon juice

salt and freshly ground black pepper

Having trawled through many traditional dishes, I discovered the wonders of a good Bercy sauce. Who needs to be trendy?

1 Place the oil and half the butter in a large frying pan over a medium heat. Season the steaks, then cook them for 3–5 minutes on each side over a medium heat, or to your liking. Remove the steaks from the pan and set aside to rest in a warm place for 5 minutes.

2 Pour the white wine into the frying pan and reduce by three-quarters. Add the stock and reduce by one-third. Remove the sauce from the heat and add the remaining butter, mixing it into the sauce by shaking the pan. Season to taste and keep warm.

3 For the Beurre Bercy, heat 25 g (1 oz) (2 tablespoons) of the butter in a pan, add the shallots and cook slowly until soft but not brown. Add the white wine and boil to reduce to 3 tablespoons. Away from the heat, add the remaining butter, the diced bone marrow, if using, chopped parsley, lemon juice and seasoning. Mix well to produce a thick, creamy butter sauce.

4 Pour the beef sauce over the steaks, then dribble 2 teaspoons of Beurre Bercy over each one. Serve with new potatoes and buttered spinach.

26 Beef Escalopes with Parma Ham, Sage and Mozzarella

Prime cut
Preparation and cooking: 30 minutes
Serves 4

4 x 175 g (6 oz) beef fillets

8 fresh sage leaves, 4 finely chopped

50 g (2 oz) (¼ cup) Parmesan cheese, freshly grated

salt and freshly ground black pepper

4 thin slices Parma ham

50 g (2 oz) (¼ cup) unsalted butter

1 tablespoon olive oil

1 ball buffalo mozzarella, cut into 8 slices

4 tablespoons dry white wine

4 tablespoons beef stock

This recipe was inspired by an Italian veal dish called saltimbocca. I find it works just as well – and is much more PC – made with beef. The melting mozzarella is my own addition to a simple flavoursome dish.

1 Place the steaks on a board, cover them with cling film and beat each one with a meat mallet or rolling pin until they are about 5 mm (¼ inch) thick.

2 Place one sage leaf in the centre of each steak, sprinkle with Parmesan, and season with a pinch of salt and a decent grinding of black pepper. Top each with one slice of Parma ham, pushing down so the ham seals itself to the steak.

3 Heat half the butter and the oil in a large, heavy-based frying pan. Cook the steaks, Parma ham side down, for 2 minutes, then turn them over and cook for a further 1 minute on the other side. Remove and set aside to keep warm, ham side up.

4 Preheat your grill. Place 2 slices of mozzarella on each steak, then grill the steaks until the cheese is melting.

5 Meanwhile, add the chopped sage to the frying pan and cook for 30 seconds. Pour in the wine and stock and boil to emulsify and reduce by half. Whisk in the remaining butter and season to taste.

6 Place a steak on each of 4 warmed plates, spoon over the sage butter sauce and serve with new potatoes and a salad.

27 Pan-fried Beef Fillet Stuffed with Chilli and Garlic

Prime cut
Preparation and cooking: 1 hour 30 minutes, plus marinating time
Serves 4

4 tablespoons extra virgin olive oil

2 heads (bulbs) garlic, unpeeled

1 small Spanish onion, unpeeled

6 large dried American chillies (Poblano or Chipotle), soaked for 1 hour in hot water, then drained

4 x 225 g (8 oz) fillet steaks

Maldon salt (sea salt) and freshly ground black pepper

4 tablespoons dry martini

150 ml (¼ pint) beef stock

1 tablespoon fresh oregano leaves

4 tablespoons double cream (heavy cream)

1 tablespoon fresh chives

If you like garlic spiced up with a few chillies then you will love this dish. Softening garlic is a great way of removing those killer-breath aromas.

1 Preheat the oven to 180°C/350°F/Gas Mark 4. Rub a little olive oil over the garlic, onion and chillies, wrap in foil and bake in the oven for 25 minutes. Remove the garlic and chillies and return the onion to the oven for another 45 minutes until very soft. Set aside to cool.

2 Press the softened garlic cloves out of their skins and place in a food processor. Peel the onion and add to the food processor with the softened chillies and half of the remaining olive oil. Blend until smooth and pass through a fine sieve to remove any chilli seeds.

3 Cut a pocket in the side of each fillet steak and spoon a small amount of garlic purée into each pocket. Allow the steaks to marinate for 1 hour, then season with Maldon salt and black pepper.

4 Heat a heavy-based frying pan until hot and pan-fry the steaks in the remaining oil until cooked to your liking: 3 minutes each side for medium-rare. Remove from the pan and keep warm. Add the dry martini to the frying pan, reduce by half over a high heat, then add the beef stock and oregano and reduce by half again. Add the cream, the remaining garlic purée and the chives and cook until the sauce is a coating consistency. Season to taste. Add any meat juices from the steaks to the sauce.

5 Place the steaks on 4 warm plates and top with the chilli and garlic sauce. Serve with your choice of vegetables.

28 Bloody Mary Steak

Prime cut
Preparation and cooking: 40 minutes, plus marinating time
Serves 2–3

2 tablespoons Worcestershire sauce

3 tablespoons fresh lemon juice

2 teaspoons fresh horseradish, grated

2 shallots, finely diced

2 teaspoons freshly ground black pepper

2 teaspoons Maldon salt (sea salt)

2 teaspoons celery salt

1 teaspoon Tabasco sauce

2 tablespoons vodka

1 x 1 kg (2 lb 4 oz) rib steak on the bone

300 ml (½ pint) tomato juice

2 teaspoons tomato purée

1 tablespoon cornflour (cornstarch)

1 tablespoon water

3 plum tomatoes, deseeded and diced

1 tablespoon fresh chives, snipped

2 tablespoons olive oil

Not many of us would decline a Bloody Mary on a Sunday morning, and this recipe puts all those spicy flavours into a wonderful rib steak.

1 Put the Worcestershire sauce, lemon juice, horseradish, shallots, pepper, salts, Tabasco and vodka in a bowl and stir to combine. Pour 3 tablespoons of the Bloody Mary mix over the steak and marinate for at least 4 hours, or ideally overnight, turning from time to time.

2 Combine the remaining Bloody Mary mix with the tomato juice and tomato purée and pour it into a saucepan over a low heat. Simmer gently for 10 minutes. Whisk together the cornflour and water and stir into the simmering sauce. Cook for 2 minutes to thicken the sauce, then fold in the tomatoes and chives. Keep warm.

3 Preheat the oven to 220°C/425°F/Gas Mark 7. Preheat an ovenproof griddle pan or frying pan, remove the steak from the marinade and pat dry. Brush the steak with the oil and sear it in the hot griddle pan or frying pan until brown on both sides. Place the steak in the hot oven and cook for 15 minutes for medium-rare, or to your liking. Remove the steak from the oven and allow to rest in a warm place.

4 Place the steak on a carving board, cut it away from the bone and slice the meat into 2.5 cm (1 inch) thick strips. Place on warm plates and spoon the sauce around the meat slices. Serve with sautéed potatoes, buttered spinach and braised celery.

29 Grilled Sirloin with Balsamic Beets and Horseradish Cream

Prime cut
Preparation and cooking: 40 minutes
Serves 4

1 teaspoon ground coriander

½ teaspoon Maldon salt (sea salt)

1 teaspoon finely ground black pepper

4 x 250 g (9 oz) sirloin steaks

a little olive oil

Horseradish Cream (for ingredients and method see page 130)

BALSAMIC BEETS

16 baby beetroot (beets)

25 g (1 oz) (2 tablespoons) unsalted butter

3 tablespoons muscovado (dark brown) sugar

75 ml (2¾ fl oz) good balsamic vinegar

4 tablespoons red wine vinegar

1 tablespoon red wine

salt and freshly ground black pepper

2 tablespoons fresh coriander leaves (cilantro)

Beef is a great accompaniment to both beetroot and horseradish, so I thought, why not combine all three..? It works a treat.

1 About 30 minutes before cooking the steaks, combine the ground coriander, salt and black pepper and sprinkle the mixture over the steaks.

2 Meanwhile, for the balsamic beets, cook the beets in boiling salted water for about 25 minutes, or until tender. Drain and return to the pan with the butter, sugar, vinegars and red wine. Cook the beets, stirring from time to time, until most of the liquid has evaporated and the beets are shiny and glazed. Season to taste and sprinkle with the coriander leaves.

3 Heat a griddle or large frying pan until almost smoking, then drizzle the pan with the olive oil. Cook the steaks for 2 minutes each side for rare, and up to 6 minutes each side for well-done. Allow the steaks to rest for 5 minutes in a warm place before serving.

4 Place each steak on a warmed plate. Top with the balsamic beets and drizzle with a little Horseradish Cream. Serve with a salad and sautéed potatoes.

30 Cajun Filet Mignon

Prime cut
Preparation and cooking: 30 minutes, plus marinating time
Serves 4–6

1 kg (2 lb 4 oz) beef fillet, centre-cut

1 small onion, grated

vegetable oil to cover the fillet

CAJUN SPICE RUB

1 teaspoon cayenne pepper

1 teaspoon ground black pepper

1 teaspoon ground white pepper

1 teaspoon chilli powder

1 teaspoon onion powder

1 teaspoon paprika

1 teaspoon garlic powder

1 teaspoon fresh thyme, very finely chopped

1 teaspoon dried basil

1 teaspoon dried oregano

¹/₂ teaspoon ground cumin

A dish from the American Deep South, where they love their spices. This adds a little excitement to a cut of meat that is tender but can be disappointing in flavour.

1 For the Cajun spice rub, combine all the herbs and spices. Lightly spike the fillet with a fork so the seasoning penetrates into the meat, then rub all over with the spice mixture. Place the meat in a glass dish, add the onion and enough oil to cover the meat. Marinate in the fridge overnight or for a minimum of 4 hours.

2 When ready to cook, remove the meat from the marinade and wipe clean. Cook the fillet in a large frying pan over a high heat for about 1 minute on each side, then continue cooking over a lower heat until cooked to your liking: about 15 minutes for rare.

3 Slice the steak thinly and arrange around a hot potato salad.

31 Mediterranean 'Minute Steak'

Prime cut
Preparation and cooking: 20 minutes, plus marinating time
Serves 6

1 tablespoon finely grated orange zest, plus 2 oranges, peeled and segmented, with the juice squeezed from the segments (retain juice and segments)

1 tablespoon fresh tarragon leaves, chopped

1 tablespoon Pernod or Ricard

8 tablespoons extra virgin olive oil

675 g (1 lb 8 oz) beef fillet steak, centre-cut, cut into 12 slices

salt and freshly ground white pepper

2 tablespoons aged red wine vinegar

3 spring onions (scallions), finely sliced on the diagonal

¹/₂ tablespoon fresh chervil, chopped

2 tablespoons fresh chives, chopped

1 tablespoon black olives, chopped

6 anchovy fillets, finely chopped

2 plum tomatoes, deseeded and diced

If you are looking for a super dish packed full of flavour, this one will bring back wonderful memories of holidays in the Med.

1 Put the orange zest, tarragon, Pernod or Ricard and 1 tablespoon of the oil in a bowl and mix together. Rub this mixture into the beef slices and marinate for 2 hours. After 2 hours, scrape the marinade off the beef and retain for later use.

2 Season the beef lightly. Heat 2 tablespoons of the oil in a frying pan and cook the beef over a high heat for 1 minute on each side. This may need to be done in batches. Remove the beef from the pan, place it on a hot platter and keep warm. Add the marinade and any juices seeping from the beef to the frying pan. Add the remaining oil, vinegar, spring onions, chervil, chives, olives, anchovies, orange juice and segments, and tomatoes. Stir together, place over a medium heat and bring to the boil. Season if necessary.

3 Divide the hot steak slices between 6 warmed plates and pour the sauce over the beef. Serve with new potatoes and peas or broad (fava) beans.

32 Grilled Teriyaki Beef

Prime cut
Preparation and cooking: 20 minutes, plus marinating time
Serves 4

4 x 250 g (9 oz) fillet or sirloin steaks

3 tablespoons vegetable oil

100 g (4 oz) (1½ cups) fresh button mushrooms, cleaned, stalks removed, and cut into quarters

4 tomatoes, deseeded and cut into thin strips

50 g (2 oz) (mung) beansprouts, washed and trimmed

50 g (2 oz) sugar snap (snow or mangetout) peas, topped, tailed and cut diagonally into 2.5 cm (1 inch) slices

2 tablespoons fresh coriander leaves (cilantro), chopped

1 tablespoon fresh mint, chopped

TERIYAKI SAUCE

150 ml (¼ pint) dark soy sauce

150 ml (¼ pint) sake

6 tablespoons mirin

3 tablespoons dark brown sugar

The sweet flavours of the teriyaki sauce penetrate the beef, making it a very moreish dish. You should always make double the quantity because your guests will be sure to want second helpings.

1 For the teriyaki sauce, mix the ingredients together in a saucepan and cook over a medium heat, stirring, until the sugar has dissolved. The sauce can be used immediately or cooled and refrigerated for later use.

2 Marinate the beef in the teriyaki sauce for 2 hours. After 2 hours, drain the steaks, reserving the sauce, and pat them dry.

3 Meanwhile, heat a little of the oil in a frying pan and fry the mushrooms, tomatoes, beansprouts and sugar snap peas for 2 minutes, until they are cooked through but still crisp. Add 2 tablespoons of teriyaki sauce, the coriander and mint and cook for a further 1 minute. Remove from the pan and keep warm.

4 Wipe the frying pan with a paper towel and add a little more oil. Fry the steaks over a medium heat for 2 minutes, until slightly browned, then turn gently and brown the other side. Be careful not to overcook the beef.

5 Drain off any excess oil from the pan and discard. Pour a little teriyaki sauce over the beef and continue to cook for a couple of minutes, turning and basting the steaks so that they are well coated and glazed.

6 To serve, remove the beef from the pan and place on individual plates. Simmer the remaining teriyaki sauce until it is thick and syrupy; be careful not to over-reduce it as it burns easily. Spoon the sauce over the beef and serve immediately with the warm vegetables.

33 Chopped Peppered Beef with Chives and Garlic

Prime cut
Preparation and cooking: 45 minutes, plus resting time
Serves 2–4

450 g (1 lb) sirloin or beef fillet, finely hand-chopped

salt

50 g (2 oz) black peppercorns, crushed

600 ml (1 pint) beef stock

16 cloves garlic, peeled

1 teaspoon fresh thyme leaves

4 tomatoes, deseeded and diced

3 tablespoons fresh chives, chopped

50 g (2 oz) (¼ cup) butter

A variation on a burger, this dish is served with a great sauce made with garlic that creates a perfect marriage of flavours.

1 Sprinkle the beef with salt and shape into patties 10 cm (4 inches) in diameter and 4 cm (1½ inches) thick, as loosely as possible but still neatly and firmly packed. Coat both sides of the 'burgers' with the crushed peppercorns and then set aside to rest for 1 hour.

2 Meanwhile, heat the stock in a saucepan, add the garlic, thyme and ½ teaspoon salt, and poach the garlic for about 20 minutes, until just tender when stuck with a fork. Strain the liquid into a bowl, reserving the garlic, then return the liquid to the pan and reduce to 150 ml (¼ pint).

3 Heat a griddle or frying pan over a high heat. Sear the 'burgers' and the poached garlic for 2 minutes on each side. Reduce the heat and cook for a further 2 minutes on each side for medium-rare, or to your liking. Remove the burgers and the garlic and keep warm.

4 Pour off all the fat from the frying pan and deglaze the pan with the garlic poaching stock. Add the tomato, chives and butter to the pan over a high heat and shake the pan to emulsify the sauce.

5 Put the burgers on warmed plates and place the garlic cloves around them. Spoon a little sauce over each burger. Serve with frites (French fries) and a salad.

34 Chopped Steak with Pinenuts and Sultanas

| Prime cut |
| Preparation and cooking: 20 minutes |
| Serves 2 |

50 g (2 oz) (¼ cup) unsalted butter

1 onion, finely chopped

1 clove garlic, mashed to a paste with a little salt

350 g (12 oz) sirloin steak with fat, finely hand-chopped

½ teaspoon sweet paprika

2 slices of day-old white bread, soaked in milk for 30 minutes then squeezed dry

1 tablespoon Parmesan cheese, grated

1 egg yolk, lightly beaten

1 tablespoon toasted pinenuts, roughly chopped

1 tablespoon sultanas (golden raisins)

1 tablespoon fresh flat-leaf parsley, chopped

½ teaspoon Dijon mustard

½ teaspoon finely ground black pepper, not powdered

½ teaspoon Maldon salt (sea salt)

1 tablespoon olive oil

8 sage leaves

Chopped steak is another name for an upmarket burger. The pinenuts, sultanas, herbs and cheese give this one some lovely textures and flavours.

1 Heat half the butter in a frying pan and cook the onion and garlic slowly until soft but not brown. Remove the onions and garlic and set aside to cool. Leave the cooking juices in the pan.

2 Combine the cooked onions and garlic with the steak, paprika, bread, Parmesan, egg yolk, pinenuts, sultanas, parsley, mustard, pepper and salt. Form into 4 large or 8 small 'burgers'. Refrigerate until ready to cook.

3 Add the remaining butter to the frying pan with the oil and sage leaves, place over a highish heat, then add the 'burgers' and seal them all over. Reduce the heat and cook the burgers to your liking: 2–3 minutes each side for medium-rare; 5 minutes each side for well-done. Serve with frites (French fries) and a tomato and onion salad.

35 Inverted Cheeseburger

Good-value cut
Preparation and cooking: 50 minutes
Serves 4

1 head (bulb) garlic, unpeeled

2 teaspoons olive oil

50 g (2 oz) ($\frac{1}{2}$ cup) Roquefort cheese

50 g (2 oz) ($\frac{1}{4}$ cup) unsalted butter

1 tablespoon fresh chives, snipped

650 g (1 lb 7 oz) minced (ground) beef (18 per cent fat)

1 tablespoon Dijon mustard

4 teaspoons coarsely ground black pepper

salt

4 burger buns

50 g (2 oz) ($\frac{1}{4}$ cup) Parmesan cheese shavings

Baby Gem lettuce (crunchy lettuce, such as romaine)

2 tomatoes, sliced

red onion rings

large sweet pickled cucumbers, sliced lengthways

tomato ketchup and mayonnaise, to serve

A cheeseburger with a difference, as you will find a wonderful Roquefort butter in the centre of the burger. Always a winner.

1 Preheat the oven to 180°C/350°F/Gas Mark 4. Cut 1 cm ($\frac{1}{2}$ inch) off the top of the head of garlic, dribble the cut surface with a little olive oil, wrap in foil and bake in the oven for 20–30 minutes until soft. Allow to cool, then separate the cloves and push out the garlic pulp using the back of a knife. Place the pulp in a bowl, dribble with olive oil and set aside until needed.

2 Mash together the Roquefort cheese, butter and chives and set aside. Combine 2 teaspoons of the garlic pulp with the minced beef and mustard and mix thoroughly. Divide the beef into 4, then form into 2.5 cm (1 inch) thick burgers. Divide the cheese butter into 4. Make a deep indentation in each of the burgers and place a nugget of butter into each, folding the beef back around the butter until it is totally sealed. Sprinkle 1 teaspoon of pepper over each burger and refrigerate until ready to cook.

3 Grill, pan-fry or barbecue the burgers to your liking: 4 minutes each side for rare; 6 minutes each side for medium-rare; 8–9 minutes each side for well-done. Season with salt.

4 Toast the cut sides of the burger buns under a grill. Place the two halves of a bun on each plate. On one half place some lettuce, tomato slices, onion rings and pickled cucumber slices, then the burger on top and some shavings of Parmesan. Serve with thin-cut chips (fries) and offer tomato ketchup and mayonnaise.

36 Aubergine Cannelloni with a Minced-Beef Filling

Good-value cut
Preparation and cooking: 2 hours 30 minutes, plus refrigeration time
Serves 4

2 large aubergines (eggplants)

salt and ground black pepper

100 g (4 oz) (4–5 slices) streaky bacon, cut into pieces

150 ml (¼ pint) good olive oil

1 each onion, celery stalk and carrot, finely sliced

2 cloves garlic, finely chopped

1 teaspoon fresh soft thyme leaves

1 bay leaf

1 teaspoon dried oregano

1 x 200 g (7 oz) can chopped tomatoes

2 teaspoons tomato purée

2 teaspoons anchovy essence (extract)

1 tablespoon Worcestershire sauce

225 g (8 oz) minced (ground) beef

150 ml (¼ pint) dry red wine

300 ml (½ pint) beef stock

50 g (2 oz) (¼ cup) Parmesan cheese, grated

RUSTIC TOMATO SAUCE

for ingredients and method see page 141

For me, aubergines are one of the nicest vegetables around, but you really have to cook them through to get that characteristic melting mouthful. If you don't have time to make my Rustic Tomato Sauce, tomato passata could be used instead.

1 Slice each aubergine lengthways into 8 slices, then sprinkle these with a little salt and leave for 30 minutes. Rinse, drain and pat dry, then set aside. Make the Rustic Tomato Sauce (see page 141) and set aside.

2 In a large, heavy-based saucepan, fry the bacon in 2 tablespoons olive oil. When the bacon is crispy and has released some natural fats, add the onion, celery, carrot, garlic, thyme, bay leaf and oregano and cook over a medium heat until the vegetables have softened and taken on a little colour. Add the canned tomatoes, tomato purée, anchovy essence and Worcestershire sauce. Stir to combine.

3 Meanwhile, in a large frying pan, heat a little olive oil and fry off the mince in small batches until browned. While the meat is frying, break up any lumps with the back of a wooden spoon. After each batch is cooked, add the meat to the bacon and vegetable mix.

4 Deglaze the frying pan with some of the red wine, scraping any crusty bits from the bottom of the pan. Pour this wine, the remaining wine and the stock into the meat saucepan. Bring to the boil, then reduce the heat and simmer, stirring from time to time, for about 1 hour. Season to taste. If the liquid reduces too much, top up with water. When the meat is tender, allow to cool, then refrigerate. When cold, lift off any solidified fat and discard.

5 Preheat the oven to 180°C/350°F/Gas Mark 4. Heat a griddle pan, brush the aubergine strips with a little seasoned olive oil and cook for 4–5 minutes, turning once, until a deep golden colour. Remove and lay on a paper towel to soak up any excess fat. Lay two aubergine strips flat on a surface, slightly overlapping, and spread the cold beef filling in the centre. Roll up into a cylinder, tucking in the ends, and place in a buttered baking dish. Repeat this process until you have 8 aubergine rolls. Pour over the Rustic Tomato Sauce, sprinkle with half the Parmesan cheese and bake in the oven for 25 minutes, until bubbling and the cheese has melted. Serve hot with a green salad and offer extra Parmesan.

37 Mini Meatballs in Red-Wine Sauce

Good-value cut
Preparation and cooking: 1 hour 45 minutes
Serves 4

5 tablespoons red wine

4–5 tablespoons double cream (heavy cream)

6 tablespoons fresh breadcrumbs

50 g (2 oz) (¼ cup) unsalted butter

1 onion, finely chopped

1 egg

450 g (1 lb) minced (ground) beef

1 tablespoon fresh chives, chopped

salt

pinch ground cloves

white pepper

2 tablespoons fresh parsley, chopped, to serve

fresh Parmesan cheese, grated, to serve

RED-WINE SAUCE

25 g (1 oz) (2 tablespoons) white flour

250 ml (9 fl oz) beef stock

250 ml (9 fl oz) red wine

250 ml (9 fl oz) fresh cream

salt and freshly ground black pepper

A very easy supper dish packed full of flavour, with lovely hints of red wine.

1 Place the red wine and cream in a bowl, add the breadcrumbs and soak for 30 minutes. Heat half the butter in a non-stick frying pan. Add the onion and pan-fry over a low heat for about 8 minutes until soft and translucent. Remove from the pan and allow to cool.

2 In a separate bowl, mix the onion and soaked breadcrumbs with the egg, minced beef and chives and season with salt, cloves and pepper. With wet hands, form the mixture into little balls, about 1 cm (½ inch) in diameter.

3 Heat the remaining butter in a large non-stick frying pan and fry the meatballs until a dark golden colour on all sides. Remove from the pan with a slotted spoon and keep warm.

4 For the red-wine sauce, stir the flour into the fat in the meatball frying pan and brown it a little. Stir in the stock and red wine and whisk to combine. Add the cream and allow the sauce to cook, covered, for approximately 10 minutes. Season to taste. Add the meatballs and simmer gently for 45 minutes, or until the sauce has thickened and the meatballs are thoroughly cooked and tender. Serve over buttered pasta and scatter with chopped parsley and grated Parmesan.

38 Beef, Tomato and Mozzarella Lasagne

Good-value cut
Preparation and cooking: 2 hours
Serves 8

1 red onion, peeled and diced

4 cloves garlic, crushed to a paste with a little salt

4 tablespoons olive oil

8 large plum tomatoes, peeled, deseeded and roughly diced

1 x 200 g (7 oz) can tomatoes

1 tablespoon tomato purée

1 bay leaf

1 tablespoon mixed fresh herbs (parsley, thyme and basil), chopped

pinch crushed chilli flakes

salt and ground black pepper

1 teaspoon fresh oregano, finely chopped

1 tablespoon fresh flat-leaf parsley, chopped

1 tablespoon fresh basil leaves, chopped

250 g (9 oz) (1 cup) ricotta cheese

1 x 375 g packet oven-cook lasagne sheets (no pre-cooking required)

450 g (1 lb) Mainstay Mince (see page 93)

100 g (4 oz) (½ cup) Parmesan cheese, freshly grated

100 g (4 oz) (1 cup) buffalo mozzarella, finely chopped

This recipe uses Mainstay Mince (see page 93) and is loved by kids and adults alike. It's an ideal dish for freezing and enjoying at a later date.

1 In a saucepan, sweat off the onion and garlic in the olive oil over a medium heat for 2–3 minutes, until soft but not brown. Add the diced tomatoes, canned tomatoes (chopped), tomato purée, bay leaf, mixed herbs and the chilli flakes. Simmer gently for about 1 hour. Purée the mixture through a food mill or food processor and season to taste.

2 Preheat the oven to 180°C/350°F/Gas Mark 4. Add the oregano, parsley and basil to the ricotta and mix well.

3 In a 25 x 15 x 5 cm (10 x 6 x 2 inch) ovenproof dish, begin to assemble the lasagne. Spread a thin layer of the tomato sauce over the base of the dish. Cover this with sheets of pasta, spread a little mince over the pasta, and top with another layer of the tomato sauce. Sprinkle with a little grated Parmesan and mozzarella. Cover with more pasta and tomato sauce and then spread half the ricotta mixture evenly over the top. Repeat with a layer of pasta, mince, tomato sauce, Parmesan and mozzarella, and then another layer of pasta, tomato sauce and the remaining ricotta mixture. Finish with a top layer of pasta, mince, tomato sauce and Parmesan and mozzarella.

4 Cover the lasagne with foil and bake in the oven for 20 minutes. Remove the foil and cook for a further 20 minutes until the top is golden and crispy. Serve with a green salad and some warm crusty bread.

39 Iranian Beef Pilaff

Good-value cut
Preparation and cooking: 1 hour, plus soaking time
Serves 4–6

1 litre (1³/₄ pints) beef stock

3 tablespoons sugar

salt and freshly ground black pepper

300 g (10 oz) (1¼ cups) long grain rice

2 tablespoons olive oil

750 g (1 lb 10 oz) rump steak, cut into 2.5 cm (1 inch) cubes

4 onions, roughly chopped

85 g (3 oz) (¹/₂ cup) raisins

100 g (4 oz) (²/₃ cup) dried apricots, chopped

1 tablespoon grated orange rind

50 g (2 oz) (¹/₂ cup) toasted flaked almonds

100 g (4 oz) (¹/₂ cup) unsalted butter

2 tablespoons fresh coriander leaves (cilantro), chopped

1 tablespoon fresh parsley, chopped

Anything with rice seems to be popular with the children, but this dish has loads of flavour and is great one-pot dining.

1 Put 700 ml (1¼ pints) stock into a bowl and stir in the sugar and 1 teaspoon salt. Add the rice and leave to soak for 30 minutes.

2 Preheat the oven to 180ºC/350ºF/Gas Mark 4. Heat the olive oil in a large frying pan and pan-fry the beef until brown all over. This may be done in batches, if necessary. Remove the beef from the pan and set aside. Add the onions to the frying pan and cook for 10 minutes until soft but not brown.

3 Put the onion and the meat into a casserole dish and mix well together. Drain the rice, discarding the soaking liquor, and mix with the raisins, apricots, grated orange rind and toasted flaked almonds. Spread the rice mixture on top of the meat and onions in a thick layer. Pour over the remaining stock. Dot the top of the rice with butter and season with salt and pepper.

4 Cover the casserole dish loosely with buttered greaseproof paper (wax paper) and then with a lid. Cook in the oven for 30–40 minutes, stirring 2 or 3 times to prevent the rice hardening. If the rice seems to be drying too fast, add more stock, little by little, around the edges of the dish, and dab some more butter on top. Sprinkle with the coriander and parsley and serve with a tomato and onion salad.

40 Quick Beef in Thai-Style Red Curry

Prime cut
Preparation and cooking: 1 hour
Serves 4

2 tablespoons vegetable oil

675 g (1 lb 8 oz) rump steak, cut into 2.5 cm (1 inch) pieces

12 shallots, thinly sliced

6 cloves garlic, finely chopped

2 tablespoons fresh ginger, grated

75g (2½ oz) (¼ cup) Thai red curry paste

2 x 400 ml (14 fl oz) cans coconut milk

1 tablespoon soft brown sugar

3 Kaffir (wild) lime leaves, thinly sliced

2 tablespoons lime juice

20 fresh basil leaves, ripped

3 handfuls washed spinach

1 tablespoon fish sauce (*nam pla*)

1 bunch fresh coriander leaves (cilantro)

1 bunch spring onions (scallions), trimmed and thinly sliced

2 green chillies, deseeded and sliced

If you like Thai green chicken curry, then you are going to like this dish. Make it as hot or as mild as you wish by adjusting the quantity of chillies and curry paste.

1 Heat the oil in a frying pan and brown the beef all over. Remove the meat from the pan and set aside. Add the shallots and garlic to the pan and cook over a medium heat until the onions start to brown. Add the ginger and curry paste and cook for 3 minutes, stirring continuously.

2 Return the beef to the pan and add one can of coconut milk, the sugar and the lime leaves. Cook over a low heat for about 40 minutes until the beef is tender. The sauce will have split (curdled), but this is normal.

3 Add the remaining can of coconut milk, lime juice, basil leaves, spinach and *nam pla* and cook for a further 5 minutes, stirring to combine. Garnish with the coriander, spring onions and chillies, and serve with fragrant rice such as jasmine.

41 Spiced Beef Curry with Spinach and Yoghurt

Good-value cut
Preparation and cooking: 2 hours 30 minutes, plus marinating time
Serves 4–6

750 g (1 lb 10 oz) chuck steak, cut into 2.5 cm (1 inch) pieces

1 thumb-size piece of fresh ginger, peeled and roughly chopped

4 cloves garlic

2 each red and green chillies, deseeded

1 x 500 g (1 lb 2 oz) tub Greek (10% butterfat content) yoghurt

2 teaspoons cumin powder

50 ml (2 fl oz) vegetable oil

1 cinnamon stick

3 black cardamom pods, crushed

3 cloves

350 g (12 oz) (3 cups) onions, roughly chopped

1 teaspoon ground coriander

1 x 400 g (14 oz) can chopped tomatoes

1 tablespoon tomato purée

salt and freshly ground black pepper

200 g (8 oz) frozen spinach, defrosted and puréed

4 plum tomatoes

1 x 225 g (8 oz) bag of baby spinach (about 4 cups)

This is a perfect way of producing melt-in-the-mouth spicy beef without it being too hot.

1 Soak the beef in warm water for 15 minutes to lighten the colour. Meanwhile, purée the ginger, garlic and chillies in a blender. Add the yoghurt to the purée, together with 1 teaspoon of cumin powder. Marinate the beef in this mixture for at least 4 hours or preferably overnight.

2 Heat the vegetable oil in a cooking pot with the cinnamon stick, cardamom pods and cloves. When the oil is really hot and the cinnamon begins to fry, add the onions. Fry for 15 minutes over a low to moderate heat until soft and lightly brown.

3 Add the ground coriander and cook for 2 minutes, stirring continuously. Add the remaining cumin powder and a couple of tablespoons of water. Allow the spices to cook.

4 Add the meat and its marinade and cook over a moderate heat for 15 minutes, stirring continuously. Then add the canned tomatoes and tomato purée and cook for a further couple of minutes. Add 350 ml (12 fl oz) hot water and a little salt. Turn the heat to low, cover with a lid and leave to simmer.

5 When the meat is almost done – about 1½ hours – add the puréed spinach and fresh tomatoes. Cook for 10 minutes, uncovered, and remove the cinnamon stick. Season to taste, fold in the baby spinach leaves and cook until wilted. Serve with plain rice.

42 Asian Massaman Beef Curry

Good-value cut
Preparation and cooking: 2 hours 15 minutes
Serves 6

75 ml (2½ fl oz) groundnut (peanut) oil or vegetable oil

1 kg (2 lb 4 oz) skirt or bavette steak, cut into 5 cm (2 inch) chunks

450 g (1 lb) small new potatoes, halved but not peeled

1 aubergine (eggplant), cut into 1 cm (½ inch) pieces

1 x 400 ml (14 fl oz) can coconut milk

1 x 400 g (14 oz) can chopped tomatoes

1 teaspoon tamarind concentrate

150 ml (¼ pint) beef stock

3 tablespoons dark muscovado (dark brown) sugar

CURRY PASTE

for ingredients and method see page 141

Most of us associate curries with India, but this one, although possibly not completely authentic, comes from further east. My curry paste uses lemongrass and shrimp paste as well as the normal Indian spices. It doesn't take long to prepare; however, ready-made pastes are more widely available these days if time is short.

1 Make the curry paste (see page 141) and set aside. Heat the oil in a heavy-based saucepan, then fry the steak in batches until brown all over. Remove the meat from the pan, drain and set aside.

2 Add the potatoes and aubergine to the steak pan and cook until browned. Fold in the curry paste, stir to combine and cook for 3 minutes.

3 Return the beef to the pan together with the coconut milk, tomatoes, tamarind, stock and sugar, bring to the boil, then reduce the heat, cover and cook gently for 1 hour.

4 Uncover and cook for a further 45 minutes or until the steak is tender and the sauce has reduced. Check the seasoning and serve with jasmine rice.

43 Indonesian Beef Curry

Good-value cut
Preparation and cooking: 2 hours 30 minutes
Serves 8

3 large onions, roughly chopped

4 large cloves garlic, roughly chopped

1 tablespoon fresh ginger, chopped

4 hot, fresh red chillies

1 tablespoon *sambal oelek* (hot chilli paste)

1 stem fresh lemongrass, thinly sliced, or grated rind of 1 lemon

2 teaspoons galangal, chopped

1 handful fresh coriander leaves (cilantro)

12 fresh mint leaves

1 tablespoon ground coriander

1 teaspoon ground cumin

1 teaspoon freshly ground black pepper

1.5 kg (3 lb 5 oz) lean chuck steak, cut into 2.5 cm (1 inch) pieces

2 x 400 ml (14 fl oz) cans coconut milk

1 tablespoon tamarind paste

salt, to taste

2 teaspoons palm or brown sugar

juice of 1 lime

You will enjoy the taste of tamarind and coconut in this curry. It's an easy one to put together although, depending on the quality of the beef, it may take a little time to cook.

1 Purée the onions, garlic, ginger, chillies, *sambal oelek*, lemongrass or lemon rind, galangal, herbs and ground spices in a food processor, then set aside.

2 Put the beef into a large saucepan and add one can of coconut milk mixed with 300 ml ($\frac{1}{2}$ pint) water, and the spice mix. Bring to the boil, stirring continuously. Mix the tamarind with about 2 teaspoons salt and add to the curry. Reduce the heat and simmer gently, uncovered, for about 2 hours, until the meat is tender and the liquid has almost evaporated.

3 Add the remaining can of coconut milk and the sugar, stirring constantly. Simmer until the gravy is very thick and has reduced to a small amount. Add the lime juice and serve with steamed rice.

44 Beef, Butternut Squash and Potato Rendang

Good-value cut
Preparation and cooking: 2 hours 15 minutes
Serves 6

6 small dried red chillies

2 teaspoons cumin seeds

1 tablespoon coriander seeds

2 x 400 ml (14 fl oz) cans coconut milk

2 onions, finely chopped

1 tablespoon fresh ginger, grated

8 cloves garlic, finely chopped

3 tablespoons coriander (cilantro) roots, finely chopped

1 stalk lemongrass, minced (finely chopped)

4 Kaffir (wild) lime leaves, shredded

2 teaspoons each powdered turmeric and powdered galangal

2 red chillies, finely sliced

12 curry leaves

850 ml (1½ pints) beef stock

1 kg (2 lb 4 oz) rump steak, cut into 2.5 cm (1 inch) cubes

8 pink-fir apple potatoes (or any new potato variety)

1 small butternut squash

50 ml (2 fl oz) fish sauce (*nam pla*)

small bunch fresh coriander leaves (cilantro)

I could have done a whole book on curries. So many magical flavours can be found in the east, and all the ingredients used in this dish are widely available in our cosmopolitan society.

1 In a non-stick pan, dry-roast, separately, the dried chillies, cumin seeds and coriander seeds over a gentle heat, until fragrant. Cool, then grind separately to a fine powder.

2 In a wide, heavy-based pan, bring the coconut milk to a simmer, then add the ground spices, onions, ginger, garlic, coriander roots, lemongrass, Kaffir lime leaves, turmeric, galangal, red chillies and curry leaves and simmer gently, uncovered, for 15 minutes.

3 Add the stock and bring to the boil. Reduce the heat, stir in the beef and simmer gently for 1 hour.

4 Peel and quarter the potatoes and then peel and deseed the butternut squash. Cut the squash into 2.5 cm (1 inch) chunks and add both vegetables to the beef and simmer for a further 30 minutes, until tender. If the liquid reduces too much during cooking, add a little water to keep the meat and potato moist. By the end of cooking, most of the liquid should have been absorbed. Season with *nam pla*.

5 Stir the coriander leaves through the curry when you are ready to serve. Offer jasmine rice separately.

45 Crispy Chilli Sichuan Beef

Walk into any Chinese restaurant and you will find on the menu crispy beef with shreds of very sweet carrots – the inspiration behind this dish.

Good-value cut
Preparation and cooking: 20 minutes, plus resting time
Serves 4–6

325 g (11 oz) skirt or sirloin, cut across the grain into julienne 7.5cm x 5 mm (3 x ¼ inch)

½ teaspoon each baking powder and salt

1 teaspoon caster (fine granulated or berry) sugar

1 egg white, beaten

2 tablespoons cornflour (cornstarch)

4 cloves garlic

2 hot red chillies

2 carrots, peeled

4 spring onions (scallions), plus extra, shredded, to serve

1 litre (1¾ pints) groundnut (peanut) oil

2 teaspoons fresh ginger, finely grated

1 tablespoon Szechuan peppercorns (see Note), crushed to a powder

1 tablespoon each preserved black beans and black bean sauce

2 teaspoons each sugar and hot chilli oil

fresh coriander leaves (cilantro), to serve

green chillies, deseeded and sliced, to serve

1 Place the beef in a bowl with the baking powder, salt and sugar. Stir together and allow to rest for 2 hours in the refrigerator. Add the egg white and cornflour, stir to combine, and allow to rest for at least another 10 minutes.

2 Meanwhile, crush the garlic cloves to a paste with a little salt and very finely chop the red chillies. Cut the carrots into matchsticks and the 4 spring onions into long thin strips. Set aside.

3 Heat a wok over a high heat for 1 minute, add the oil and heat to 190°C/375°F. Add the beef with its marinade and fry for 3 minutes, separating the beef slices. Turn off the heat, remove the beef from the pan with a slotted spoon, drain, and cool to room temperature.

4 Reheat the oil to 190°C/375°F. Place the beef back in the wok and fry for 3 minutes, until crisp. Turn off the heat. Remove the beef from the pan with a slotted spoon and drain. Set aside.

5 Pour off all but 1 tablespoon of oil from the wok. Heat over a high heat for 15 seconds. Add the garlic, chopped chillies, ginger and peppercorn powder and cook, stirring, until the paste releases its fragrance.

6 Add the carrot matchsticks to the wok and cook, stirring, for 30 seconds. Add the spring onion strips and cook, stirring, for 30 seconds. Add the beef, stir to mix, and cook for 1 minute. Add the preserved black beans, black bean sauce, sugar, and hot chilli oil. Stir well and cook for 2 minutes, or until all the ingredients are well combined and hot. Turn off the heat, transfer to a heated platter, sprinkle with the shredded spring onion, coriander leaves and chilli slices. Serve with rice.

Note
Szechuan peppercorns are not usually available in America. Substitute 1½ teaspoons each black peppercorns and aniseed.

46 Dry-fried Oriental Beef

Good-value cut
Preparation and cooking: 15 minutes
Serves 4

4 tablespoons sesame oil

350 g (12 oz) rump or sirloin steak, fat removed, cut into pieces about 2.5 cm (1 inch) long x 5 mm (¼ inch) thick

2 tablespoons rice wine

1 teaspoon chilli bean paste (*toban jiang*)

1 tablespoon sweet bean sauce (*hoi sin*)

½ teaspoon chilli powder

2 cloves garlic, crushed to a paste with a little salt

1 teaspoon caster (fine granulated or berry) sugar

3 celery stalks

2 medium carrots, peeled and cut into matchsticks

1 tablespoon spring onions (scallions), finely chopped

½ teaspoon fresh ginger, finely chopped

½ teaspoon ground Szechuan peppercorns (see Note)

2 tablespoons fresh coriander leaves (cilantro), chopped

1 teaspoon chilli oil

Oriental food is incredibly popular, but for some reason we seem a little scared of attempting it at home. Give it a try – it's really quite easy and delicious.

1 Heat a wok over a high heat and add the sesame oil. Before the oil gets too hot, add the beef and half the rice wine. Stir-fry until the pieces have separated, then reduce the heat and continue stirring until the beef is dry (pour off the excess liquid, if necessary).

2 Add the chilli bean paste, sweet bean sauce, chilli powder, garlic, sugar, celery, carrots and the remaining rice wine. Increase the heat and stir-fry for 2–3 minutes. Add the spring onions, ginger, Szechuan peppercorn powder, coriander leaves and chilli oil. Stir well and serve hot with rice.

Note
Szechuan peppercorns are not usually available in America. Substitute ¼ teaspoon each black peppercorns and aniseed.

47 Aromatic Beef Stir-fry

Prime cut
Preparation and cooking: 30 minutes, plus marinating time
Serves 4

8 spring onions (scallions)

6 sun-dried tomatoes

450 g (1 lb) fillet or sirloin steak, trimmed of all fat

4 tablespoons soy sauce

2 tablespoons each cornflour (cornstarch) and soft dark brown sugar

1 tablespoon chilli oil (plus 1 teaspoon 'gloop' from chilli oil)

1 tablespoon ginger, grated

2 tablespoons garlic, chopped

1/2 teaspoon dried chilli flakes

450 ml (16 fl oz) chicken stock

2 tablespoons rice wine or dry sherry

1 tablespoon rice vinegar

350g (12 oz) green vegetables (asparagus, sugar snap (snow or mangetout) peas, broccoli florets, Chinese leaves (Chinese cabbage))

600 ml (1 pint) groundnut (peanut) oil

100 g (4 oz) (2 cups) baby spinach

4 cherry tomatoes, halved

2 tablespoons fresh basil leaves, ripped

1 tablespoon fresh coriander leaves (cilantro), chopped

The beauty of stir-fries is that they are so quick to prepare, as long as you have all the components of the dish ready before you start cooking. The chilli oil 'gloop' that I mention is the sediment of pungent and flavourful ingredients such as dried shrimp that are added to the bottle to give the oil its intense flavour. If your chilli oil doesn't have this then using just the oil is fine.

1 Cut 4 of the spring onions into 1 cm (1/2 inch) slices and the remaining 4 into 2.5 cm (1 inch) pieces. Cut the sun-dried tomatoes into strips. Set aside. Cut the beef lengthways into 5 cm (2 inch) wide strips, then cut each strip into 5 mm (1/4 inch) pieces. Combine half the soy sauce with half the cornflour, half the sugar, the chilli oil and the chilli oil 'gloop'. Fold in the beef and make sure each slice is coated with the marinade. Cover and refrigerate overnight, tossing occasionally.

2 Combine the ginger, garlic and chilli flakes and the 1 cm (1/2 inch) spring onion slices and set aside. In a separate bowl, combine the chicken stock, remaining soy sauce, remaining sugar, rice wine and rice vinegar, and set aside. Blanch the vegetables in boiling salted water (asparagus: 3 minutes; sugar snap peas: 1 minute; broccoli florets: 2 minutes; Chinese leaves cut into 2.5 cm (1 inch) pieces: 2 minutes), drain and plunge into iced water. Drain again, dry and set aside.

3 Remove the meat from its marinade. The next stage is to 'velvet' it. In a wok or deep saucepan, heat the oil to 180°C/350°F. Slide the beef into the oil and stir to separate the strips of meat. Cook for 30–45 seconds, stirring continuously, then scoop the meat out into a colander or metal sieve. Drain all but 2 tablespoons of the cooking oil from the wok into a bowl (the drained oil can be used another time).

4 Add the ginger and garlic mix to the oil in the wok and stir for 45 seconds over a high heat. Add the spinach and the remaining spring onions, and cook for 3 minutes, stirring until the spinach has wilted. Add the sun-dried and cherry tomatoes and the chicken stock mixture and bring the sauce to a simmer. Take 2 tablespoons of the liquid and combine with the remaining cornflour. Fold into the simmering sauce and cook for around 30 seconds, until the sauce becomes glossy and starts to thicken. Fold in the meat, blanched vegetables and herbs. Cook until warmed through and serve with rice or noodles.

48 Steak Cacciatore

Prime cut
Preparation and cooking: 30 minutes
Serves 4

1 tablespoon olive oil

450 g (1 lb) piece sirloin or rump steak, about 4 cm (1½ inches) thick

salt and freshly ground black pepper

350 g (12 oz) dried rigatoni pasta

2 shallots, finely chopped

2 garlic cloves, crushed

½ teaspoon fresh thyme, chopped

1 fresh bay leaf

100 g (4 oz) (4–5 slices) streaky bacon cut into small strips

400 g (14 oz) can pimentos in brine, rinsed and cut into long, thin strips

50 g (2 oz) (¼ cup) pitted black olives

350 g (12 oz) jar puttanesca (spicy tomato) sauce

100 g (4 oz) (1½ cups) mixed mushrooms, sliced

1 tablespoon fresh oregano, chopped

This easy pasta sauce can be made well in advance, then reheated gently and folded into the sliced steak before serving on a bed of the rigatoni pasta. I can honestly say that I think dried pasta is better for most recipes. It uses a hard wheat, which when cooked properly gives that lovely 'bite' that we talk about when cooking pasta.

1 Heat the oil in a heavy-based frying pan over a high heat. Add the steak and cook for 2 minutes on each side, then reduce the heat and continue to cook for 5–10 minutes, turning once, depending on how rare you like your steak. Transfer the steak to a plate, season to taste with salt and set aside in a warm place to rest.

2 Meanwhile, bring a large pan of water to a rolling boil. Add a good pinch of salt and tip in the rigatoni, stir once and cook for 8–12 minutes, or according to the packet instructions, until the pasta is *al dente*.

3 Add the shallots to the pan in which you cooked the steak, with the garlic, thyme and bay leaf. Cook for 2 minutes, stirring, then add the bacon strips and continue to cook until sizzling but not browned. Add the pimentos and olives and cook for a further 2 minutes. Stir in the puttanesca sauce and then add the mushrooms and oregano. Season and continue to cook until the mushrooms are tender, stirring occasionally.

4 Slice the rested steak on the diagonal, cutting away and discarding any fat, then return to the pan with any juices, stirring to combine with the sauce. Drain the pasta, quickly refresh under cold running water, then divide among the serving bowls. Spoon over the steak slices and sauce and serve at once.

49 Braised Beef Short Ribs

Good-value cut
Preparation and cooking: 3 hours, plus marinating time
Serves 4

2 tablespoons fresh thyme leaves, chopped

4 tablespoons olive oil

1 tablespoon orange zest

2 tablespoons garlic, chopped

2.5 kg (5 lb 8 oz) short ribs from prime or best-quality beef

salt and freshly ground black pepper

2 onions, finely chopped

2 carrots, finely sliced

2 celery stalks, finely sliced

850 ml (1½ pints) full-bodied red wine

1.4 litres (2½ pints) beef stock

1 tablespoon sherry vinegar

1 tablespoon lemon zest

1 tablespoon whole fresh tarragon leaves

1 tablespoon chilli oil

2 handfuls fresh parsley leaves

You will have to ask your local butcher to give you some chined rib bones for this dish. Cooked slowly these produce a melt-in-the-mouth result.

1 Put the thyme, 3 tablespoons olive oil, the orange zest and garlic in a bowl and mix together. Rub this marinade mixture into the ribs. Cover and marinate for at least 4 hours in the refrigerator. Remove from the refrigerator and allow to come to room temperature before cooking.

2 Preheat a frying pan to a high temperature and the oven to 150°C/300°F/Gas Mark 2. Wipe the marinade off the ribs and season them, reserving the marinade. Fry the ribs for 8 minutes on each side until golden brown.

3 Put the onions, carrots and celery in a heavy casserole dish (big enough to hold the ribs in one layer) along with the reserved marinade. Cook over a medium heat for 5 minutes, stirring constantly. Then add the ribs side by side. Add the wine to the ribs and cook over a high heat for 5 minutes. Add the stock and bring to a very low simmer. Transfer to the oven and braise, covered, for 2 hours, or until the ribs are tender.

4 Remove the ribs from the dish, put in a bowl and cover with cling film. Strain the braising liquid into a saucepan, discarding the vegetables, and simmer over a low heat, slightly off to the side of the burner, skimming off any fat and scum that rises to the top. Keep skimming the liquid and reduce it to half its original volume. Remove from the heat and pour over the ribs.

5 Put a pinch of salt and pepper into a small mixing bowl, whisk in the sherry vinegar, followed by the lemon zest, tarragon, the remaining olive oil and the chilli oil. Add the parsley leaves and toss them in the mixture. Divide the hot ribs between 4 hot plates, put the dressed parsley in the centre of the ribs and serve with mashed potatoes.

50 Braised Beef Short Ribs with Horseradish Potato Purée

Good-value cut
Preparation and cooking: 5 hours 30 minutes
Serves 4

12 short ribs, trimmed of excess fat

salt and ground black pepper

50 ml (2 fl oz) vegetable oil

1 Spanish onion, finely chopped

2 leeks, finely sliced

2 celery stalks, roughly chopped

6 cloves garlic, chopped

1 carrot, roughly chopped

2 medium-hot red chillies, deseeded and chopped

600 ml (1 pint) red wine

6 tablespoons coarsely grated fresh horseradish, plus 4 teaspoons for garnish

3 sprigs fresh rosemary

600 ml (1 pint) beef stock

85 g (3 oz) (¼ cup plus 2 tablespoons) unsalted butter

16 button mushrooms

225 g (8 oz) pancetta, cut into large lardons (or 9–10 slices smoked streaky bacon, cut into large strips)

2 tablespoons olive oil

2 tablespoons fresh flat-leaf parsley, chopped

1 kg (2 lb 4 oz) floury (starchy) potatoes, peeled and chopped

225 ml (8 fl oz) hot milk

I have included two beef short rib recipes in this chapter (the other one is on page 75) because I think it is a cut of beef worth discovering. The beef is full of flavour and melts on the bone, and is complemented perfectly by the horseradish potato purée.

1 Preheat the oven to 180°C/350°F/Gas Mark 4. Season the ribs, then heat the vegetable oil in a roasting pan over a medium-high heat and sear the ribs for 2–5 minutes on each side, or until golden brown. Remove the ribs from the roasting pan and set aside.

2 Cook the onion, leeks, celery, garlic, carrot and chillies in the roasting pan over a medium-high heat for 7–10 minutes or until golden brown. Add the red wine, 3 tablespoons grated horseradish, rosemary and beef stock and bring to a simmer. Return the ribs to the pan and cover with foil. Braise in the oven for 3–4 hours or until the meat is tender.

3 Remove the roasting pan from the oven and strain the cooking liquid into a saucepan over a medium heat. Fold in half the butter and set aside to keep warm. Set aside the ribs to keep warm.

4 Place the mushrooms and bacon lardons in an ovenproof pan with the olive oil and cover with foil. Reduce the oven heat to 140°C/275°F/Gas Mark 1 and cook for 1 hour or until tender. Toss the mushrooms and bacon with the parsley and season to taste with salt and pepper.

5 For the horseradish potato purée, cook the potatoes in boiling salted water until tender. Drain and pass through a potato ricer or *mouli-légumes*. Place the potatoes in a medium bowl with the remaining butter and grated horseradish and half the milk and whip until smooth. Whisk in the remaining milk until the mixture has a ribbon-like consistency. Season to taste.

6 Arrange some of the mushroom and bacon mix and 3 ribs in the centre of each plate. Spoon a ring of the horseradish potato purée around each plate. Spoon the red wine jus over the ribs and sprinkle with the grated horseradish.

51 Slow-cooked Beef with Ceps

Good-value cut
Preparation and cooking: 3 hours 30 minutes, plus marinating time
Serves 6–8

1.8 kg (4 lb) boneless beef chuck steak, cut into 5 cm (2 inch) pieces

3 each onions and carrots, peeled

8 sprigs fresh thyme

2 bay leaves

1 fresh rosemary sprig, about 15 cm (6 inches) long

1 teaspoon Maldon salt (sea salt)

2 tablespoons freshly ground black pepper

4 cloves garlic, peeled

2 strips orange zest, dried or fresh

1 bottle (750 ml) 'beefy' red wine

150 ml (¼ pint) brandy

175 g (6 oz) pancetta (or 7–8 slices smoked streaky bacon), cut into 1 cm (½ inch) pieces

2 tablespoons plain flour (all-purpose flour)

300 ml (½ pint) beef stock

50 g (2 oz) (1 cup) dried ceps, soaked in boiling water for 30 minutes

450 g (1 lb) wide, flat, dried pasta noodles (such as pappardelle)

Ceps, or porcini as the Italians call them, are probably the strongest-flavoured wild mushroom. I serve this beef dish with noodles instead of traditional potatoes as I think it's a nicer combination.

1 Place the meat in a large non-metallic bowl. Quarter one of the onions and add the pieces to the meat along with the carrots, thyme, bay leaves, rosemary, salt, half the pepper, two of the garlic cloves (left whole) and the orange zest. Pour the wine and brandy into the bowl and turn to mix and immerse the ingredients. Cover and marinate in the refrigerator for at least 4 hours, or preferably overnight.

2 Put the pancetta or bacon in a heavy-bottomed casserole dish large enough to hold the marinating mixture. Place the dish over a low heat and cook for about 5 minutes, stirring occasionally, until the bacon fat is released. Finely chop the remaining onions and garlic cloves, and add to the bacon. Cook over a medium heat for 6–8 minutes until translucent. Remove all solids with a slotted spoon and set aside.

3 Drain the meat, reserving the marinade and its ingredients. Pat the meat as dry as possible. Add the meat to the casserole dish a few pieces at a time and fry for about 5 minutes, turning them once or twice. The meat will darken in colour but will not really brown. Remove the pieces with a slotted spoon and repeat until all the meat has been fried. When the last of the meat pieces have been removed, add the flour to the dish and cook until it browns, stirring often. Raise the heat to high and slowly pour in the reserved marinade and its ingredients. Deglaze the dish, scraping up any bits clinging to the bottom.

4 Return the bacon and onion mixture to the dish, along with the meat and any collected juices. Add the stock, strained cep liquor and soaked mushrooms and bring almost to a boil. Reduce the heat to very low, cover with a tight-fitting lid and simmer for 2½ to 3 hours, until the meat can be cut through with a spoon and the liquid has thickened.

5 Remove from the heat. Discard the whole carrots, herb sprigs, bay leaves and onion quarters. Skim off any fat with a ladle. Season to taste.

(continued opposite)

85 g (3 oz) (¼ cup plus 2 tablespoons) unsalted butter, cut into small cubes

50 g (2 oz) (¼ cup) Parmesan cheese, grated

3 tablespoons fresh flat-leaf parsley, chopped

6 Meanwhile, bring a large pot of salted water to the boil. Add the pasta, stir well and cook until just tender. Drain the pasta, transfer to a warmed serving bowl and toss with the butter, Parmesan and parsley. Season to taste. Spoon the meat onto the pasta and serve immediately.

52 Hungarian Goulash

Good-value cut
Preparation and cooking: 3 hours 30 minutes
Serves 6–8

450 g (1 lb) onions, peeled

1 tablespoon vegetable oil

2 cloves garlic, crushed to a paste with a little salt

2 red peppers (bell peppers)

1.3 kg (3 lb) lean braising beef, such as flank or chuck, cut into 5 cm (2 inch) pieces

2 tablespoons sweet paprika, plus extra to serve

1 tablespoon flour

pinch of chilli powder or cayenne pepper

1 teaspoon caraway seeds

300 ml (½ pint) beef or veal stock

1 x 400 g (14 oz) can tomatoes

150 ml (¼ pint) red wine

salt and ground black pepper

300 ml (½ pint) soured cream

Goulash used to be a regular on bistro menus, and yet nowadays it is rarely seen. More's the pity, because the paprika and caraway seeds turn good, cheap cuts of beef into a flavour-packed casserole.

1 Slice the onions. Heat the oil in a large, heavy casserole dish and fry the onions and garlic over a medium heat until golden brown. Remove from the dish and set aside.

2 Deseed the peppers and cut into 2.5 cm (1 inch) cubes. Add the peppers and beef to the dish and cook over a medium heat until evenly browned. Sprinkle over the paprika, flour, chilli powder or cayenne pepper and caraway seeds and stir in well, continuing to cook.

3 Add a little stock and vigorously scrape off any bits stuck to the bottom of the dish. Add the rest of the stock with the tomatoes, wine, onions, garlic and seasoning. Bring to the boil, then reduce the heat, cover and simmer very gently for about 3 hours.

4 Remove the dish from the heat and add half the soured cream. Remove the meat from the dish and set aside. Liquidize the sauce, then pass through a sieve.

5 Return the meat to the sauce and serve with boiled or steamed potatoes, wide noodles or dumplings, and top with a dollop of the remaining soured cream and a sprinkling of paprika.

53 Beef and Onions Braised in Beer

Good-value cut
Preparation and cooking: 3 hours 30 minutes
Serves 4–6

800 g (1 lb 12 oz) chuck steak, cut into 5 cm (2 inch) cubes

salt and freshly ground black pepper

3 tablespoons olive oil

50 g (2 oz) (¼ cup) unsalted butter

3 large onions, peeled and thinly sliced

1 teaspoon fresh soft thyme leaves

2 bay leaves

2 tablespoons flour

600 ml (1 pint) bitter or stout (Guinness or ale)

300 ml (½ pint) beef stock

1 teaspoon brown sugar

1 tablespoon red wine vinegar

1 bouquet garni (see method for ingredients)

This is British food at its best. There are plenty of men, and possibly a few women, who would love their partner to present them with food like this on a more regular basis.

1 Season the beef with salt and pepper. Heat the oil and the butter in a heavy pan over a high heat. As soon as it is smoking, add the meat and brown on all sides. Remove the meat from the pan and set aside.

2 Add the onions to the pan and brown them lightly in the fat used to brown the meat. Add the thyme and bay leaves and stir to combine. Remove the onions and set aside. Add the flour to the pan and stir over a low flame until the resulting roux is a dark-gold colour. Pour in the beer and the stock, add a pinch of salt, a pinch of pepper, the sugar and vinegar. Bring to the boil, stirring, and simmer over a very low flame for 15 minutes.

3 Preheat the oven to 160°C/325°F/Gas Mark 3. In an earthenware casserole dish or terrine large enough to hold all the meat, place the meat and the onions in layers. Put the bouquet garni in the centre. Strain the sauce through a very fine sieve on to the meat, cover and cook in the oven for 3 hours, until the meat is tender and the sauce reduced and slightly thickened.

4 Remove from the oven and discard the bouquet garni. Allow to stand for a few minutes and skim off the fat. Correct the seasoning of the sauce and serve in the cooking pot with some mashed potatoes and greens.

To make a home-made bouquet garni
Take 2 strips of leek, 2 fresh thyme sprigs, 4 fresh parsley stalks and 2 fresh bay leaves, and tie neatly between 2 sticks of celery with some string. Alternatively, you can buy a packet of bouquet garni from your supermarket.

54 Oxtail Stew with Buttered Macaroni

Good-value cut
Preparation and cooking: 4 hours, plus marinating time, over 3 days
Serves 6

2.5 kg (5 lb 8 oz) oxtail, cut into 10 cm (4 inch) pieces

300 g (10 oz) salt pork or (12–14 slices) streaky bacon

2 tablespoons olive oil

50 g (2 oz) (½ cup) seasoned flour

450 g (1 lb) each baby carrots and peeled baby onions

1 x 400 g (14 oz) can chopped tomatoes

salt and ground black pepper

1 handful fresh flat-leaf parsley

450 g (1 lb) uncooked macaroni

50 g (2 oz) (¼ cup) unsalted butter, cut into cubes

MARINADE

4 cloves

450 g (1 lb) onions, peeled

1 head (bulb) garlic, cloves peeled and halved

450 g (1 lb) carrots, peeled and cut into 2 cm (¾ inch) slices

1 bottle gutsy red wine

1 bunch fresh parsley

4 bay leaves

6 sprigs fresh thyme

1 teaspoon black peppercorns

This dish seems to have got lost in culinary time, which is a pity as it's a wonderful winter warmer served with macaroni instead of the usual mash or new potatoes.

1 For the marinade, quarter the onions and stick a clove into 4 of the onion pieces. Place all of the marinade ingredients in a large non-metallic casserole dish. Add the oxtail pieces. Cover and refrigerate overnight, stirring from time to time. When marinated, remove the pieces of oxtail and drain well (retaining the marinade). Dry the oxtail with kitchen roll (paper towel) and set aside.

2 Cut the salt pork or bacon into 2.5 cm (1 inch) pieces. Heat the olive oil in a heavy saucepan over a medium-high heat, add the salt pork or bacon and cook until evenly browned. Remove from the pan and set aside. Dust the oxtail with the seasoned flour and add to the pan in batches, cooking until evenly browned.

3 Return the salt pork to the pan, add the marinade and its ingredients and enough water to cover generously. Bring to a simmer over a medium heat. Carefully skim off any grease or impurities that rise to the top. Keep the mixture simmering gently for at least 3 hours until the meat is falling off the bone. Remove the oxtail, bacon and bay leaves from the pan and liquidize the remaining sauce, then pass through a fine sieve. Return the oxtail and bacon to the sauce, cool and refrigerate overnight.

4 The next day, remove and discard any fat that has solidified on top of the stew. Return the stew to a pan, add the baby carrots, onions, tomatoes and seasoning, bring to a simmer and cook for 30 minutes, or until the carrots and onions are tender and heated through. Season to taste. Chop the flat-leaf parsley and fold in to the stew.

5 Bring a large pan of salted water to the boil. Add the macaroni and cook until *al dente*, then drain well. Toss the macaroni with the butter, season and divide evenly between 6 shallow soup bowls.

6 Carefully remove the pieces of oxtail from the stew. Drain and place on a carving board. Remove the meat in big chunks and place them on top of the macaroni. Spoon the sauce and the vegetables over the meat, season and serve.

55 Beef in Stout with Dumplings

Good-value cut
Preparation and cooking: 4 hours
Serves 6–8

2 tablespoons sunflower oil

50 g (2 oz) (¼ cup) unsalted butter

1.8 kg (4 lb) chuck or blade beef steak, cut into 5 cm (2 inch) pieces

1 heaped tablespoon plain flour (all-purpose flour)

salt and freshly ground black pepper

225 g (8 oz) bacon lardons (or 10–12 slices bacon, cut into small strips)

450 g (1 lb) shallots, peeled

1 tablespoon Dijon mustard

2 tablespoons dark muscovado (dark brown) sugar

175 g (6 oz) (1½ cups) ready-to-eat prunes, cut in half

175 g (6 oz) (1 cup) pickled walnuts, cut into quarters

1 litre (1¾ pints) stout (such as Guinness)

850 ml (1½ pints) fresh beef stock (from a carton is fine, or canned beef consommé)

1 bouquet garni (see Tip on page 80)

DUMPLINGS

see method for ingredients

Hints of Britain find their way into this wonderfully warming one-pot supper. Serve with bowls of glazed carrots and steamed leeks.

1 Preheat the oven to 140°C/275°F/Gas Mark 1. Heat the oil and butter in a large non-stick frying pan. Place the beef in a large bowl and sprinkle over the flour and seasoning. Toss until lightly coated, shaking off any excess. Add half the beef to the pan and cook over a medium heat until the meat is lightly browned. Then transfer the beef with a slotted spoon to a casserole dish. Repeat with the remaining beef.

2 Add the bacon lardons to the frying pan and cook until sizzling and golden brown. Remove and set aside. Add the shallots and cook for another 2–3 minutes, stirring.

3 Meanwhile, add the mustard, sugar, prunes and pickled walnuts to the beef in the casserole dish, then tip in the bacon lardons and shallots, stirring to combine. Pour about a quarter of the stout into the frying pan and allow to bubble down, scraping the bottom of the pan to remove any sediment. Pour into the casserole dish, then stir the rest of the stout and the beef stock into the casserole dish.

4 Add the bouquet garni to the casserole and season to taste. Bring to the boil, then cover and place in the oven. Cook for 2–3 hours until the beef is completely tender but still holding its shape. In the meantime, make the dumplings (see below).

5 Remove the cooked stew from the oven, season to taste and place the dumplings on top. Increase the oven temperature to 180°C/350°F/Gas Mark 4. Return the casserole to the oven and cook, uncovered, for another 35–40 minutes until the dumplings have risen and are golden brown. Remove the bouquet garni, sprinkle with parsley (reserved from the dumplings) and serve.

To make the Dumplings
Sift 250 g (9 oz) (2¼ cups) plain flour (all-purpose flour), 1 teaspoon salt and 2 teaspoons baking powder into a large bowl. Make a well in the centre and add 2 tablespoons olive oil and 4 tablespoons each chopped fresh flat-leaf parsley (keeping some aside to garnish) and snipped fresh chives. Pour in 150 ml (¼ pint) milk and, using a fork, mix to form a soft dough. Place the dough on a lightly floured surface, knead briefly and shape into 16 walnut-sized dumplings.

Warming winter dishes

56 Braised Beef with Pickled Walnuts and Celery

Good-value cut
Preparation and cooking: 3 hours 15 minutes
Serves 4

4 x 300 g (10 oz) braising steaks

seasoned flour, for dusting

50 g (2 oz) (¼ cup) dripping (fat from roasted meat) or oil

100 g (4 oz) (½ cup) button onions

150 ml (¼ pint) red wine

600 ml (1 pint) beef stock

2 sprigs fresh thyme

2 sprigs fresh parsley

2 cloves garlic, crushed with a little salt

salt and freshly ground black pepper

100 g (4 oz) (1½ cups) clean whole button mushrooms

4 pickled walnuts, halved

2 celery hearts, halved lengthways

25 g (1 oz) (2 tablespoons) butter

1 teaspoon grated orange peel, to serve

1 tablespoon fresh parsley, chopped, to serve

This slow-cooked dish uses a good-value cut of beef that picks up the wonderful flavours of the pickled walnuts and celery.

1 Dust the steaks with seasoned flour. Heat the dripping or oil in a frying pan and fry the meat over a medium-high heat until browned all over. Remove the steaks from the pan and set aside. Add the onions to the pan and fry gently until golden.

2 Return the meat to the pan with the onions, then add the wine, stock, herbs and garlic. Season with salt and pepper, cover and simmer over a very low heat for 1½ hours. Then add the mushrooms, walnuts and celery. Cover and cook for a further 1½ hours.

3 Whisk in the butter, season to taste and sprinkle with orange peel and chopped parsley. Serve with buttery mashed potatoes.

57 Steak-and-Kidney Pudding

Good-value cut
Preparation and cooking: 5 hours 20 minutes, plus chilling time
Serves 6–8

750 g (1 lb 10 oz) chuck or blade beef steak, cut into 2.5 cm (1 inch) cubes

225 g (8 oz) ox kidney, cut into 2.5 cm (1 inch) cubes

1 small onion, finely chopped

large pinch of celery salt

1 teaspoon fresh thyme leaves

salt and freshly ground black pepper

2 tablespoons plain flour (all-purpose flour)

150 ml ($^1/_4$ pint) fresh beef stock (from a carton is fine, or canned beef consommé)

SUET PASTRY

400 g (14 oz) self-raising flour (to make your own, use 3$^1/_2$ cups all-purpose flour plus 5$^1/_4$ teaspoons baking powder and 1$^3/_4$ teaspoons salt), plus extra for dusting

$^1/_2$ teaspoon salt (omit if you are making the self-raising flour from scratch)

200 g (7 oz) beef or vegetarian suet (or 1 cup less 2 tablespoons lard or shortening)

300 ml ($^1/_2$ pint) cold water

unsalted butter, for greasing

I love a pudding even though it requires a little attention. Some make it with a cooked-meat filling, but I prefer to make it from scratch to allow the wonderful juices to soak into the suet pastry.

1 Place the steak and kidney in a large bowl. Stir in the onion, celery salt, thyme and seasoning. Toss together lightly and set aside, or cover with cling film and chill for up to 24 hours to allow the flavours to combine.

2 For the suet pastry, sift the flour and salt (if using) into a bowl. Add the suet, some pepper and mix lightly. Then add the water a little at a time, cutting through the mixture with a round-bladed knife. Use your hands to form a soft dough.

3 Roll out the pastry on a lightly floured work surface into a round disc approximately 5 mm–1 cm ($^1/_4$–$^1/_2$ inch) thick. Cut out a quarter wedge of the pastry and set aside for the lid. Use the remainder of the pastry to line a well-buttered 1.7 litre (3 pint) pudding basin (Pyrex bowl), leaving at least 1 cm ($^1/_2$ inch) of the pastry hanging over the edge.

4 Add the flour to the steak-and-kidney mixture and stir gently to combine. Place batches of the meat mixture into a sieve over a bowl and shake to remove any excess flour. Spoon the lightly coated mixture into the lined pudding basin, being careful not to press it down, then pour in enough of the beef stock to reach about two-thirds of the way to the top, but not covering the meat completely.

5 Roll out the pastry lid to a circle 2.5 cm (1 inch) larger than the top. Dampen the edges of the pastry lining the basin, place the lid over the filling and press both edges together to seal. Trim off any excess pastry and make two small slits in the top. Cover the pudding with a double piece of buttered foil, pleated in the centre to allow room for expansion while cooking. Secure it with string, making a handle so that you can lift it out of the steamer.

6 Place the pudding on an upturned (upside-down) plate in a large pan filled two-thirds up the side of the basin with water. Steam for 5 hours, adding boiling water occasionally so as not to allow the pan to boil dry. Cut the string from the pudding basin and remove the foil. Wrap it in a folded clean white napkin to serve with bowls of mashed potatoes and buttered peas.

58 Beef Chilli For a Crowd with Chilli Crème Fraîche

Good-value cut
Preparation and cooking: 3 hours 20 minutes, plus refrigeration time
Serves 10–12

2 tablespoons olive oil

2 kg (4 lb 8 oz) coarsely minced (ground) beef

450 g (1 lb) (18–20 slices) streaky bacon, cut into strips

1 kg (2 lb 4 oz) onions (about 6 cups, chopped)

1 tablespoon garlic, 3 celery stalks and 4 chillies, finely diced

1 bay leaf

2 tablespoons each ground oregano leaves and ground cumin

1 tablespoon each ground coriander and fennel seeds

½ tablespoon paprika

1 tablespoon each cayenne pepper (or to taste), and unsweetened cocoa powder

1 teaspoon powdered cinnamon

2 x 400 g (14 oz) cans tomatoes

300 ml (½ pint) beef stock

2 tablespoons tomato purée

1 tablespoon black pepper

3 x 400 g (14 oz) cans dried red kidney beans

1 handful fresh coriander leaves (cilantro)

CHILLI CRÈME FRAÎCHE

see method for ingredients

This chilli recipe has won several awards. It's easy to make and perfect for one of those big bashes where you need a little food to soak up the alcohol.

1 Heat the oil in a large saucepan and brown the minced beef over a light heat, working in batches if necessary. Remove the beef from the pan and set aside.

2 Add the bacon to the pan and fry until golden. Finely dice the onion and add to the pan with the garlic, celery, chillies, bay leaf, herbs and spices. Cook until softened and brown.

3 Return the meat to the pan and add the cocoa powder, cinnamon, canned tomatoes (chopped), stock, tomato purée and black pepper. Cover and simmer for 2½ hours over a low heat. Top up with more stock if it becomes too dry.

4 Drain and rinse the kidney beans and add them to the pan. Cook for a further half an hour, keeping them covered with juices.

5 Fold in the coriander leaves just before serving. Serve with chopped red onions and the Chilli Crème Fraîche.

To make the Chilli Crème Fraîche

You will need 350g (12 oz) (1½ cups) crème fraîche (sour cream). To this add 1 teaspoon chilli powder, ½ teaspoon ground cumin, 3 tablespoons lime juice, 3 tablespoons each fresh chopped coriander (cilantro) and fresh chopped parsley. Blend together and refrigerate overnight.

59 Peach-Bourboned Meatballs

Good-value cut
Preparation and cooking: 50 minutes
Serves 8

1.3 kg (3 lb) minced (ground) beef

300 ml (½ pint) milk

50 g (2 oz) (1 cup) fresh white breadcrumbs

1½ tablespoons Worcestershire sauce

2 teaspoons salt

2 cloves garlic, finely chopped

½ teaspoon ground nutmeg

½ teaspoon ground ginger

½ teaspoon freshly ground black pepper

1 teaspoon Tabasco sauce

50 g (2 oz) (¼ cup) unsalted butter

BOURBON PEACH SAUCE

1½ tablespoons cornflour (cornstarch)

1 tablespoon water

450 g (1 lb) (1½ cups) peach conserve or jam

200 g (7 oz) (1 cup, less 2 tablespoons firmly packed) soft brown sugar

150 ml (¼ pint) bourbon

150 ml (¼ pint) (½ cup) orange marmalade

¼ teaspoon nutmeg

I discovered this recipe in a Chicago restaurant, although the use of bourbon means it came from further south. Nicely spiced, with lots of sweetness, it's one the kids will like – as long as you remember to cook out the bourbon to remove the alcohol!

1 In a bowl, blend together all the meatball ingredients except the butter and shape the mixture into balls about 2.5 cm (1 inch) in diameter. Heat the butter in a frying pan and fry the meatballs over a medium-high heat until brown all over. Remove from the pan and set aside.

2 Combine all the bourbon peach sauce ingredients and add to the meat fat from cooking the meatballs. Bring to a simmer and cook for 10 minutes. Add the meatballs to this sauce and simmer for 30 minutes.

3 Remove the meatballs and set aside. If the sauce is not thick, blend a little more cornflour with some water and add to the sauce, stirring constantly, cooking until thick. Return the meatballs to the sauce and serve with rice, pasta or mashed potatoes.

Variation
Make smaller meatballs, remove them from the sauce after cooking and serve on cocktail sticks with the sauce separately for dipping.

60 Twice-cooked Beef with Mustard and Breadcrumbs

Good-value cut
Preparation and cooking: 3 hours 45 minutes
Serves 4

4 x 300 g (10 oz) beef braising steaks

seasoned flour, for dusting

50 g (2 oz) (¼ cup) lard or 2 tablespoons olive oil

85 g (3 oz) (3–4 slices) streaky bacon, cut into small pieces

1 onion, finely diced

1 carrot, peeled and finely diced

1 celery stalk, finely sliced

2 tablespoons fresh soft thyme leaves, finely chopped

1 tablespoon orange zest

2 bay leaves

2 tablespoons garlic, chopped

150 ml (¼ pint) red wine

1.2 litres (2 pints) beef stock

4 tablespoons Dijon mustard

175 g (6 oz) (2½ cups) white breadcrumbs

85 g (3 oz) (¼ cup, plus 2 tablespoons) unsalted butter, melted

salt and freshly ground black pepper

Old-fashioned braised beef is lovely, but this is a way of enjoying meltingly tender beef with a nice crispy, spicy topping

1 Preheat the oven to 150°C/300°F/Gas Mark 2. Dust the steaks with seasoned flour. Heat the lard or oil in a large casserole dish and fry the steaks over a high heat until golden on both sides. Remove from the pan and set aside.

2 Add the bacon, onion, carrot, celery and half the thyme to the beef pan, reduce the heat and cook for about 10 minutes until lightly caramelized, stirring from time to time.

3 Return the beef to the pan, add the orange zest, bay leaves, garlic, red wine and stock and bring to the boil. Cover with a tight-fitting lid and place in the oven. Cook for about 3 hours, or until the beef is tender. Remove from the oven and allow to cool.

4 Increase the oven heat to 190°C/375°F/Gas Mark 5. Remove the beef from the braising liquor, wipe dry, then brush both sides of the steaks with a liberal coating of mustard. Combine the breadcrumbs with the melted butter and remaining thyme, and season. Pat the breadcrumbs onto both sides of the steaks, place on a roasting tray and cook in the oven for 20–30 minutes until the beef is heated through and the breadcrumbs are golden.

5 Meanwhile, strain the cooking juices and discard the solids. Place the juices in a pan over a medium heat and reduce until a coating consistency. Serve the beef with fluffy mashed potatoes, buttered cabbage and the sauce separately.

61 Beef Tagine with Jewelled Couscous

Good-value cut

Preparation and cooking:
3 hours 20 minutes, plus
refrigeration time

Serves 6–8

1 teaspoon cayenne pepper

2 teaspoons each ground black
pepper and ground cinnamon

3 teaspoons ground turmeric

1½ tablespoons each ground
ginger and paprika

1 kg (2 lb 4 oz) chuck steak

3 tablespoons olive oil

1 head (bulb) garlic, peeled and
crushed to a paste with some salt

450 g (1 lb) (2½ cups) onion,
grated

175 g (6 oz) (1 cup) dried
apricots, soaked in a little water

85 g (3 oz) (¾ cup) flaked almonds

50 g (2 oz) (⅓ cup) sultanas
(golden raisins) or raisins

1 tablespoon clear honey

1 teaspoon saffron stamens,
soaked in cold water

600 ml (1 pint) each tomato
juice and beef stock

1 x 400 g (14 oz) can tomatoes

chopped rind of 1 pickled lemon

25 g (1 oz) (⅓ cup) fresh
coriander (cilantro), chopped

JEWELLED COUSCOUS

for ingredients and method
see page 140

You rarely find beef used in tagines in Morocco, but as a Brit who likes to play with food I asked myself why we shouldn't use it in this country. It makes a delicious stew and wears spicy flavours well. My Jewelled Couscous is a great accompaniment; however, pre-mixed packets of couscous are increasingly available in supermarkets and taste quite good. If you haven't time, one of these would be a suitable alternative.

1 Combine the cayenne pepper, black pepper, cinnamon, turmeric, ginger and paprika in a small bowl, then tip half into a large bowl. Cut the beef into 5 cm (2 inch) cubes and add the pieces to the mixture in the large bowl. Toss until evenly coated and refrigerate overnight.

2 Preheat the oven to 160°C/325°F/Gas Mark 3. In a heavy saucepan, brown the beef in 2 tablespoons of the olive oil over a high heat, working in batches if necessary. Remove and set aside. Add the remaining spice mix, garlic and grated onion to the pan. Cook for about 8 minutes until the onions are softened but not browned.

3 Add the apricots and their soaking water, almonds, sultanas or raisins, honey, saffron, tomato juice, beef stock and tomatoes (roughly chopped). Bring to the boil, cover, then transfer to the oven and cook for 2½–3 hours. In the meantime, make the Jewelled Couscous (see page 140).

4 Remove the beef from the oven. If the sauce is not of coating consistency, remove the solids and set aside, then reduce the sauce in a pan over a high heat until thickened.

5 Fry the lemon rind in the remaining olive oil for a few minutes, then fold in the coriander.

6 Combine the sauce with the beef, if necessary, and scatter with the lemon and coriander. Serve with the Jewelled Couscous.

62 Mexican-style 'Boiled Beef' with Salsa Verde

Good-value cut
Preparation and cooking: 4 hours 15 minutes over 2 days, plus refrigeration time
Serves 10

5.6 litres (10 pints) water or beef stock

1 bouquet garni (see method for ingredients)

2 each turnips and onions, peeled and chopped

2 heads (bulbs) garlic, halved

small bunch fresh coriander (cilantro)

small bunch flat-leaf parsley

1 kg (2 lb 4 oz) marrow beef bones (ask your butcher to cut them into 2.5 cm (1 inch) pieces)

1 kg (2 lb 4 oz) beef shin, cut into 2.5 cm (1 inch) sections

1.5 kg (3 lb 5 oz) chuck steak, cut into 7 cm (2¾ inch) chunks

1 teaspoon salt

6 carrots, peeled

1 large butternut squash, peeled

3 ears of corn

6 courgettes (zucchini)

6 spring onions (scallions)

50 g (2 oz) green chillies

225 g (8 oz) (1 cup) cooked chickpeas

1 large bunch fresh coriander leaves (cilantro)

Salsa Verde (see page 131)

I love *bollito misto* and *pot-au-feu*, which in essence are just boiled meats. This Mexican offering adds some different flavours, making boiled beef a touch special.

1 Bring the water or stock to the boil. Add the bouquet garni, turnips, onions, garlic and herbs. Return to the boil and add the beef bones, shin, chuck and the salt. Return to the boil over a medium heat. Skim thoroughly. Reduce the heat and simmer for 3½ hours, skimming whenever necessary.

2 Remove the vegetables, herbs and bones and leave the beef to cool in the broth, then refrigerate. The next day, skim off any fat that has formed.

3 Reheat the broth 30 minutes before you are ready to eat. Cut the carrots into large chunks and the butternut squash into 2.5 cm (1 inch) chunks. After 5 minutes' reheating the broth, add the carrot and squash chunks and simmer for 25 minutes. Cut the ears of corn into 4 pieces each and, halfway through the cooking time, add them to the broth. Cut the courgettes into large chunks and add these 8 minutes before serving.

4 To serve, pour the broth into a soup tureen. Finely slice the spring onions and deseed and chop the chillies. Arrange the beef in the centre of a large heated platter, garnish with the cooked vegetables and scatter with the spring onions, chillies, chickpeas, and coriander. Serve with rice or new potatoes and the Salsa Verde (see page 131).

To make a home-made bouquet garni
Take 2 sprigs fresh mint, 6 bay leaves, 4 sprigs fresh thyme and 4 sprigs fresh marjoram and tie into a neat bundle with string.

63 Mainstay Mince

Good-value cut
Preparation and cooking: 2 hours 30 minutes
Makes 2 kg (4 lb 8 oz)

225 g (8 oz) (9–10 slices) streaky bacon, cut into small pieces

175–200 ml (6–7 fl oz) good olive oil

2 onions, finely diced

2 celery stalks, finely diced

2 carrots, peeled and finely sliced

5 cloves garlic, peeled and crushed with a little salt

2 teaspoons fresh soft thyme leaves

2 bay leaves

2 teaspoons dried oregano

2 x 400g (14 oz) cans chopped tomatoes

2 tablespoons tomato purée

1 tablespoon anchovy essence (extract)

2 tablespoons Worcestershire sauce

1.8 kg (4 lb) minced (ground) beef

250 g (9 oz) fresh chicken livers, finely chopped

2 bottles dry red wine

1.7 litres (3 pints) chicken, beef or lamb stock

salt and freshly ground black pepper

This mince (ground beef) dish provides a myriad of opportunities for creating meals such as bolognese, cannelloni, shepherd's pie, moussaka, lasagne and good old boiled mince and mashed potatoes. A wonderful standby worth making in large quantities and freezing. You can split the quantity from this recipe into 9 parts – each to serve 2 – and freeze.

1 In a large heavy-based saucepan, fry the bacon in 2 tablespoons of olive oil over a medium-high heat. When the bacon is crisp and has released some natural fats, add the onion, celery, carrots, garlic, thyme, bay leaves and oregano and cook over a medium heat until the vegetables have softened and taken on a little colour. Add the canned tomatoes, tomato purée, anchovy essence and Worcestershire sauce. Stir to combine.

2 Meanwhile, in a large frying pan, heat a little olive oil and fry off the mince in small batches until browned. While the meat is frying, break up any lumps with the back of a wooden spoon. Repeat, using more oil each time if necessary, until all the meat is used up. After each batch, add the meat to the sauce mix.

3 In the same frying pan, fry the chicken livers until brown and crusty (in a little more olive oil) and add the livers to the meat. Deglaze the frying pan with some of the red wine, scraping any crusty bits from the bottom, then pour this wine mixture, the remaining wine and the stock into the meat pot.

4 Bring to the boil, reduce the heat and simmer, stirring from time to time, for about 2 hours. Season to taste. If the liquid reduces too much, top up with water. When the meat is tender, allow to cool, then refrigerate. When cold, lift off the solidified fat and discard. Freeze the mixture in small batches.

64 Caribbean Jerk Steak

Prime cut
Preparation and cooking: 30 minutes, plus marinating time
Serves 4

4 hot red chillies, deseeded and roughly chopped

2 tablespoons ground allspice

$\frac{1}{2}$ teaspoon ground cinnamon

$\frac{1}{8}$ teaspoon ground nutmeg

1$\frac{1}{2}$ teaspoons smoked paprika

1 teaspoon salt

1 teaspoon freshly ground black pepper

6 spring onions (scallions), roughly chopped

4 cloves garlic, sliced

2 tablespoons white wine vinegar

4 tablespoons olive oil

4 x 280 g (10 oz) rib-eye steaks

One of my favourite holiday destinations is Jamaica, and it was there that I tasted decent jerk seasoning for the first time. Give this one a try.

1 Place all the ingredients except the steaks in a food processor and blend until they form a paste.

2 Spread 2 tablespoons of the paste over each steak, coating both sides, cover with cling film and allow to marinate overnight or for at least 4 hours.

3 Remove the steaks from the fridge at least half an hour before you wish to cook them. Grill, barbecue or pan-fry the steaks over a fierce heat for 3–4 minutes for medium-rare, or to your liking. Allow to rest for 5 minutes on a warm plate.

4 In a pan, heat the remaining paste, adding water to achieve your desired sauce consistency and serve with the steak alongside slices of griddled or oven-roasted pineapple and roasted sweet potato wedges.

65 Steak, Kidney and Mushroom Pie

Good-value cut
Preparation and cooking: 3 hours 10 minutes
Serves 6

675 g (1 lb 8 oz) chuck steak, cut into 3 cm (1¼ inch) pieces

225 g (8 oz) kidney, cut into 1 cm (½ inch) pieces

25 g (1 oz) (¼ cup) seasoned flour

25 g (1 oz) (2 tablespoons) dripping (fat from roasted meat)

225 g (8 oz) (2 cups) onions, finely chopped

100 g (4 oz) (1½ cups) whole clean button mushrooms

½ teaspoon soft fresh thyme leaves

1 bay leaf

600 ml (1 pint) beef stock

1 tablespoon fresh parsley, chopped

325 g (11 oz) puff pastry

1 egg, beaten

Unlike steak-and-kidney pudding, which is usually cooked from raw, the steak-and-kidney pie filling is cooked before topping it with the pastry crust. I prefer puff pastry, but by all means use shortcrust pastry if you wish.

1 Roll the beef and kidney in the seasoned flour and shake to remove the excess flour.

2 Heat the dripping in a heavy-based saucepan, add the beef and kidney pieces – this may need to be done in batches – and cook over a high heat until browned all over. Remove from the pan and set aside.

3 Add the onions, mushrooms, thyme and bay leaf to the pan and cook over a medium heat for about 12 minutes until the onions have browned. Return the meat to the pan and stir to combine. Add the stock, bring to the boil, then reduce the heat and simmer gently for 2 hours, stirring from time to time and topping up with more stock as necessary: the sauce should be the consistency of single cream (half-and-half cream).

4 Remove from the heat, discard the bay leaf, fold in the parsley, allow to cool and refrigerate until ready to use, if necessary.

5 Meanwhile, preheat the oven to 180°F/350°C/Gas Mark 4. Put the meat mixture into a 1.7 litre (3 pint) pie dish. Roll out the pastry to cover the top of the dish and place on top of the meat. Brush the pastry with the beaten egg and make a small slash in the top to allow steam to escape. Place in the oven and cook for 45 minutes until deep golden brown.

66 Alternative Low-carb Cottage Pie

Good-value cut
Preparation and cooking: 1 hour
Serves 4

4 tablespoons olive oil, for cooking, plus olive oil spray

1 large onion, finely chopped

1 tablespoon plain flour (all-purpose flour)

2 fresh bay leaves

1 teaspoon fresh thyme, chopped

1 teaspoon anchovy essence (extract)

1 x 200 g (7 oz) can chopped tomatoes

250 ml (8 fl oz) fresh lamb, chicken or beef stock (from a carton is fine, or canned beef consommé)

2 teaspoons Worcestershire sauce

450 g (1 lb) lean minced (ground) beef

1 medium cauliflower, broken into florets

2 tablespoons low-fat Greek yoghurt (or any low-fat yoghurt)

1 egg yolk

salt and freshly ground black pepper

2 tablespoons fresh wholegrain breadcrumbs

Traditionally, shepherd's pie was made from lamb, while cottage pie was made from any leftover roasts. My Alternative Low-carb Cottage Pie is a little different as you are replacing the potatoes with cauliflower. Delicious.

1 Heat half the olive oil in a frying pan, add the onion and cook over a low heat for 8 minutes until softened but not browned, stirring occasionally. Add the flour and stir to combine, then add the bay leaves, thyme, anchovy essence, chopped tomatoes, stock and Worcestershire sauce and bring to the boil, stirring from time to time.

2 Meanwhile, heat a large, heavy-based pan. Add the remaining 2 tablespoons olive oil, then add half of the minced beef and cook over a fairly high heat until evenly browned, breaking up any lumps with a wooden spoon. Transfer the cooked beef to the sauce. Repeat for the remaining beef. (If you can't find lean mince, cook the mince and allow to cool. When it has formed a hard crust of fat on the top, lift it off with a spatula.)

3 Place the cauliflower in a pan of boiling salted water, cover and simmer for 15–20 minutes, or until tender. Drain and return to the pan for a couple of minutes to dry out, shaking the pan occasionally to prevent the cauliflower sticking to the bottom. Place the cauliflower in a food processor and blend until smooth. Transfer to a large bowl and beat in the yoghurt and egg yolk. Season to taste.

4 Preheat the oven to 180°C/350°F/Gas Mark 4. Spoon the beef mixture into a 1.7 litre (3 pint) pie dish, discarding the bay leaves. Cover with the mashed cauliflower, then smooth over with a spatula. Top with the breadcrumbs and spray with a little olive oil. Bake for 25–30 minutes or until bubbling and golden brown. Serve at once straight from the dish with a bowl of peas.

67 'Posh' Fajitas with Guacamole

Prime cut
Preparation and cooking: 15 minutes, plus marinating time
Serves 4–6

675 g (1 lb 7 oz) beef fillet, centre-cut, cut into 1 cm (¹/₂ inch) slices

3 cloves garlic, crushed to a paste with a little salt

juice and grated zest of 2 unwaxed lemons

1¹/₂ teaspoons ground cumin

1 teaspoon ground coriander

¹/₂ teaspoon cayenne pepper

2 tablespoons extra virgin olive oil

1 jar wood-roasted red peppers (bell peppers), drained and cut into strips, to serve

1 jar wood-roasted artichokes, drained and cut into quarters, to serve

1 jar hot chunky tomato salsa, to serve

soured cream, to serve

12 small soft, flour tortillas

GUACAMOLE

see method for ingredients

If you go to a 'Mexican' restaurant in the UK the fajitas tend to be a concoction of all sorts of odds and sods including refried beans. This version is a little more upmarket – and a little healthier.

1 Place the beef fillet slices into a bowl and combine with the garlic, lemon juice and zest, cumin, coriander, cayenne pepper and olive oil. Refrigerate and allow to marinate for at least 3 hours.

2 Heat a griddle pan or barbecue and cook the fillet slices quickly in batches to your liking.

3 Place the meat on a platter, and put the roasted peppers, artichokes, salsa, guacamole (see below) and soured cream into separate bowls. Take a little of each and roll everything up in a soft tortilla.

For the guacamole
Roughly mash the flesh of 2 large avocados. Fold in ¹/₂ teaspoon each of ground cumin and ground coriander. Deseed and dice 2 plum tomatoes and add these plus 2 tablespoons lime juice and 1 teaspoon Tabasco sauce to the mixture. Then, add 1 small finely chopped red onion, 2 tablespoons roughly chopped coriander leaves (cilantro) and 2 tablespoons extra virgin olive oil. Season to taste, cover with cling film and set aside until ready to serve.

68 'French' Shepherd's Pie

Good-value cut
Preparation and cooking: 1 hour 45 minutes
Serves 8

2 tablespoons olive oil

1.5 kg (3 lb 5 oz) lean beef, freshly chopped

225 g (8 oz) lean salt pork (or 8–10 slices bacon), cut into small pieces

3 onions, peeled and chopped

salt and ground black pepper

3 bay leaves

2 handfuls fresh flat parsley leaves, chopped

4 garlic cloves, peeled and crushed with a little salt

1 egg, lightly beaten

1 tablespoon fresh chives, snipped

1 teaspoon fresh soft thyme leaves

2 kg (4 lb 8 oz) floury (starchy) potatoes, peeled and cut into 5 cm (2 inch) cubes

3 tablespoons butter, plus extra for cooking

300 ml (½ pint) warm milk

300 ml (½ pint) warm double cream (heavy cream)

freshly ground nutmeg

225 g (8 oz) (2 cups) Gruyère cheese, grated

3 tablespoons white breadcrumbs

If you like shepherd's pie, as most of us do, then try this classic, often called *Hachis Parmentier*. Instead of one layer of potatoes on top, the potatoes are layered throughout the dish and topped with some cheese and breadcrumbs.

1 Heat the oil in a large frying pan or saucepan and fry the beef over a medium-high heat until evenly browned, breaking up any lumps with a wooden spoon. Pour the beef into a dish and set aside.

2 Add the salt pork or bacon to the frying pan. Cook for a few minutes, until crisp, then add to the beef. Add the onions to the frying pan. Sprinkle with salt, add the bay leaves and cook for about 10 minutes, over a low heat, until soft.

3 Add the onion mixture to the beef and bacon, discarding the bay leaves, and mix in the parsley, garlic, beaten egg, chives and thyme. Check and correct the seasoning.

4 Heat a large pan of salted water. Add the potatoes and cook for about 20–25 minutes until soft. Drain and allow the potatoes to dry. Mash the potatoes while they are warm, using either a *mouli-légumes* or potato ricer. Fold in the butter and add the warm milk and cream little by little until creamy (you may not need all the cream). Check and correct the seasoning, adding nutmeg, salt and pepper to taste.

5 Butter a large gratin dish. Pour a layer of potato purée over the bottom of the dish, followed by a layer of the meat mixture, and repeat, finishing with a top layer of potato purée. Pat the top of the dish with your wet hands or the back of a spoon. Sprinkle over the grated cheese and breadcrumbs and dot with butter. Refrigerate until ready to cook.

6 Take the gratin dish out of the refrigerator an hour before cooking. Preheat the oven to 180°C/350°F/Gas Mark 4. Place the shepherd's pie in the oven and cook for about 1 hour, or until bubbling and golden. Serve with a well-dressed green salad.

69 Carpetbag Steaks

Prime cut
Preparation and cooking: 30 minutes
Serves 4

4 x 225 g (8 oz) beef fillet steaks, centre-cut

8 oysters

pinch of mace

salt and freshly ground black pepper

50 g (2 oz) (¼ cup) unsalted butter

splash of Worcestershire sauce

splash of Tabasco sauce

1 tablespoon olive oil

1 glass white wine

150 ml (¼ pint) beef stock

2 teaspoons fresh tarragon, chopped

Surf and turf at its best. I have adapted the original recipe by pan-frying the oysters before I stuff them into the fillet, as this enables you to eat the rare meat but still know that the oysters are cooked.

1 Using a sharp knife, make a deep horizontal slit in the centre of the fillet steaks, taking care not to separate them into two halves.

2 Remove the oysters from their shells and sprinkle each with a little mace and pepper. Heat half the butter in a frying pan and pan-fry the oysters for 30 seconds each side until the edges start to curl. Splash with the Worcestershire and Tabasco sauces and remove from the heat, then allow the oysters to cool.

3 Stuff each fillet with two oysters and secure the openings with cocktail sticks, or sew them up with butchers' twine (or kitchen string). Fold over tightly so that the oysters are enclosed.

4 Heat the oil in a large frying pan and brown the meat all over. Cook over a gentle heat for 3–6 minutes each side, depending on how you like your steak cooked. Remove the steaks from the pan and allow to rest for 5 minutes in a warm place.

5 Deglaze the frying pan with the white wine, scraping any crusty residue from the bottom of the pan. Reduce the liquid by half then add the stock and tarragon, stirring to emulsify. Finally, thicken the sauce by adding the remaining butter. Check and correct the seasoning.

6 Place the steaks on 4 warm plates and spoon a little of the sauce over each one. Serve with mashed potatoes and peas.

70 Steak in Garlic Sauce with Cheesy Potatoes

Good-value cut
Preparation and cooking: 50 minutes
Serves 6

6 x 250 g (9 oz) sirloin steaks

salt and freshly ground black pepper

18 cloves garlic, 16 unpeeled, 2 peeled and finely chopped

300 ml (½ pint) double cream (heavy cream)

1 kg (2 lb 4 oz) floury (starchy) potatoes, peeled and thinly sliced

300 ml (½ pint) milk

1 teaspoon fresh soft thyme leaves

6 tablespoons unsalted butter

100 g (4 oz) (1 cup) Gruyère cheese, grated

2 tablespoons Parmesan cheese, grated

2 tablespoons brandy

75 ml (2½ fl oz) dry white wine

450 ml (16 fl oz) beef stock

Garlic is so *de rigueur* these days that it's surprising it hasn't yet reached the pudding stage. It is, however, well suited to this delicious steak dish.

1 Preheat the oven to 180°F/350°C/Gas Mark 4. Sprinkle the steaks with salt and pepper and set them aside at room temperature. Place the unpeeled garlic cloves on a baking sheet (cookie sheet) and place them in the oven for 15 minutes. When they are cool enough to handle, pop the cloves out of their skins and blend the pulp with half the cream. Set aside.

2 Cook the potatoes in the milk and the remaining cream, with the thyme, the 2 cloves chopped garlic and half the butter, for 12 minutes, or until the potatoes are tender. Tip them into a buttered gratin dish and sprinkle with the cheeses. Place the dish under a grill and cook until the top is brown and bubbling.

3 In a frying pan, heat the remaining butter, and when it is hot, add the steaks. Sear them over a high heat and cook for about 2 minutes each side for medium-rare, or to your liking.

4 Remove the steaks from the pan and keep them warm. Deglaze the pan with the brandy and then with the wine. Add the beef stock and reduce the mixture by half. Add the garlic cream, simmer for 5 minutes, and adjust the seasoning to taste. Serve the steaks with the potatoes, topped with the sauce and accompanied by a green vegetable.

71 Skirt Steak with Red Wine and Shallots

Good-value cut
Preparation and cooking: 30 minutes
Serves 2

50 g (2 oz) (¼ cup) butter

3 shallots, peeled and cut into fine rings

½ teaspoon fresh soft thyme leaves

175 ml (6 fl oz) red wine

1 tablespoon olive oil

2 x 225 g (8 oz) skirt steaks

salt and freshly ground black pepper

175 ml (6 fl oz) beef stock

50 g (2 oz) bone marrow (optional), poached and cut into 5 mm (¼ inch) dice

2 tablespoons fresh parsley, chopped

Supermarkets seem to have forgotten that this cut of meat exists so you will have to go to your local butcher to find it. The trick is to cook it very fast as overcooking produces a very tough piece of meat which then needs to be braised to render it tender again.

1 Heat half the butter in a heavy-based frying pan, add the shallots and thyme and cook until the shallots are golden brown. Add 125 ml (4 fl oz) wine and transfer the mixture to a saucepan. Simmer slowly until the liquid is reduced by half. Set aside.

2 Wipe the frying pan dry, add the olive oil and heat until very hot. Season the steaks well and cook for about 2 minutes on each side: they will cook quite quickly and are easily overcooked. Remove the steaks from the pan and transfer to a warm plate. Do not let them sit in their juices as they release them, but do save the juices.

3 Add the stock and remaining wine to the hot frying pan, scrape up the juices and boil until well reduced. Add the shallot sauce, the bone marrow, if using, and the parsley. Season to taste and pour in the juice from the steaks. Whisk the remaining butter into the sauce, return the steaks to the pan to warm through very briefly, and serve immediately with new potatoes.

72 Individual Beef Pies

Good-value cut

Preparation and cooking:
40 minutes, plus
refrigeration time

Makes 6 pies

**450 g (1 lb) Mainstay Mince
(for ingredients and method
see page 93)**

**125 g (4 oz) (¾ cup) frozen
peas, defrosted**

3 sheets ready-rolled puff pastry

**2 tablespoons tomato ketchup
(optional)**

1 egg, lightly beaten

Yet another way of using Mainstay Mince (see page 93). Everyone loves this simple dish, so don't just save it for half-time at the football ground!

1 Combine the mince with the peas and set aside. Preheat the oven to 190°C/375°F/Gas Mark 5.

2 Cut 2 circles (approximately 13 cm (5 inches) in diameter) from opposite corners of each sheet of puff pastry. Cut 2 circles (approximately 9 cm (3½ inches) in diameter) from the remaining corners of each sheet of pastry. Place the larger circles in 6 holes of a large non-stick muffin tray (muffin pan) to cover the base and sides; trim off any excess pastry. Prick the bottoms of each pastry case and cover with baking paper. Refrigerate, along with the small circles, for half an hour.

3 Fill each lined pastry case with uncooked rice or baking (dry) beans and bake in the oven for 12 minutes. Remove the baking paper and rice or beans and allow the pastry to cool.

4 Spoon the mince and peas into the cooked cases. Top each with a little ketchup, if using. Brush the edges of the pastry with a little of the beaten egg. Top the filled pies with the smaller pastry circles, pressing the edges together to seal. Brush the tops with the remaining beaten egg.

5 Bake the pies in the oven for about 20–25 minutes until puffed and golden. Serve hot with buttery mashed potatoes.

73 Spicy Meatballs in a Butternut Squash Casserole

Good-value cut
Preparation and cooking: 50 minutes, plus refrigeration time
Serves 4

MEATBALLS

450 g (1 lb) minced (ground) beef

1 onion, finely chopped then cooked in butter until soft

1 clove garlic, chopped

2 teaspoons ground cumin

1 teaspoon ground coriander

$\frac{1}{2}$ teaspoon sea salt

pinch of cayenne pepper

2 tablespoons fresh coriander leaves (cilantro), chopped

flour, for coating

4 tablespoons olive oil

BUTTERNUT SQUASH CASSEROLE

2 tablespoons olive oil

1 onion, roughly chopped

2 cloves garlic, finely chopped

1 red pepper (bell pepper), deseeded and chopped

1 chilli, deseeded and finely diced

1 teaspoon fresh thyme leaves, finely chopped

1 small butternut squash

salt and ground black pepper

1 tablespoon fresh mint, chopped

Kids love meatballs, and this dish has the added advantage of introducing them to a sweet vegetable – butternut squash – which, in my opinion, is underused.

1 For the meatballs, place the minced beef, onion, garlic, ground cumin, ground coriander, sea salt, cayenne pepper, and coriander leaves into a food processor and blend until smooth. Using your hands, take a small handful of the mixture and roll it into a ball, then place it on a lightly floured tray. Repeat this process until you have used up all the mixture. Refrigerate until ready to cook, ideally for at least 2 hours.

2 Roll the meatballs in flour until coated. Heat the oil in a frying pan and shallow-fry the meatballs until golden all over, remembering to turn during cooking. Drain the meatballs on kitchen paper (paper towels) and set aside.

3 Meanwhile, for the squash casserole, heat the olive oil in a deep frying pan, add the onion, garlic, pepper, chilli and thyme leaves and cook until the onion is softened but not coloured. Peel and deseed the butternut squash, and cut into 1 cm ($\frac{1}{2}$ inch) cubes. Add these to the casserole and cook, stirring frequently, for about 10 minutes, or until the squash is nearly cooked.

4 Add the meatballs and cook for a further 20 minutes. Season with salt and pepper, then fold in the chopped mint. Serve with warm pitta (pita) breads, a little salad and a dollop of Greek yoghurt (or sour cream).

74 Beef Hash Browns

Good-value cut
Preparation and cooking: 20 minutes
Serves 6–8

450 g (1 lb) minced (ground) beef

100 g (4 oz) (4–5 slices) smoked streaky bacon, cut into small pieces

4 tomatoes, peeled, deseeded and chopped

1 onion, finely chopped

50 g (2 oz) (¼ cup) unsalted butter, melted

2 cloves garlic, finely chopped

2 tablespoons sherry vinegar

1 tablespoon Dijon mustard

450 g (1 lb) peeled floury (starchy) potatoes, grated

1 teaspoon Maldon salt (sea salt)

½ teaspoon finely ground black pepper

50 g (2 oz) (¼ cup) beef dripping (fat from roasted meat) or olive oil

Worcestershire sauce, to taste

fried or poached eggs, to serve

In America, beef hash browns are usually made from salt beef or pickled beef, but I have adapted this recipe to use minced beef. It's a great brunch dish, especially topped with a fried or poached egg.

1 Combine all the ingredients except the dripping and Worcestershire sauce. Heat the dripping in a large frying pan and cook the hash over a high heat for about 10 minutes, stirring frequently.

2 Reduce the heat and cook for about a further 10 minutes until the potatoes are tender and the hash is brown and crispy all over. The secret to a good hash is to keep breaking up the mixture and stirring the brown, crispy bits into the centre.

3 Season with Worcestershire sauce and serve a large spoonful of hash with a fried or poached egg.

75 Italian Meatloaf with Cab Gravy and Whipped Corn Potatoes

Good-value cut
Preparation and cooking: 1 hour 30 minutes, plus soaking time
Serves 8–10

MEATLOAF

25g (1 oz) (½ cup) dried porcini mushrooms

85 g (3 oz) (¼ cup plus 2 tablespoons) unsalted butter

½ onion, finely chopped

5 spring onions (scallions), finely chopped

2 celery stalks, finely diced

1 large carrot, finely diced

½ each green pepper and red pepper (bell pepper), finely diced

2 teaspoons garlic, mashed with a little salt

100 g (4 oz) chicken livers

2 teaspoons salt

75 ml (2½ fl oz) each piri-piri sauce and tomato ketchup

2 teaspoons ground black pepper

½ teaspoon each cumin and nutmeg

75 ml (2½ fl oz) each milk and double cream (heavy cream)

450 g (1 lb) each minced (ground) beef and minced (ground) pork

3 large free-range eggs, beaten

85 g (3 oz) (1¾ cups) soft breadcrumbs

I was introduced to this dish in Robert De Niro's restaurant on the west coast of America – his chef agreed to part with the recipe and I have since made a few adaptations. An old-fashioned dish that is always popular.

1 For the meatloaf, soak the porcini in 300 ml (½ pint) of boiling water for 20 minutes, then rinse under cold running water to remove any grit. Retain the soaking liquor and strain through muslin to remove any grit or dust. Squeeze the porcini dry and chop finely.

2 Heat the butter in a frying pan over a medium heat and pan-fry the onions, celery, carrot, green and red peppers, garlic and chopped mushrooms until the vegetables are soft but not brown. Remove from the heat, tip into a large bowl and allow to cool. Meanwhile, finely dice the chicken livers. Fold the liver pieces plus the remaining meatloaf ingredients into the cooled vegetable mixture. Mix well to combine. Test the seasoning by frying a small amount of the mixture and tasting the sample; adjust if necessary.

3 Preheat the oven to 180°C/350°F/Gas Mark 4. Transfer the meatloaf mixture to a greased loaf tin (pan). Set the tin in a larger pan and pour enough water into the larger pan to reach halfway up the sides of the loaf tin. Bake in the oven for about 1 hour, or until the internal temperature of the meatloaf comes to 65°C/150°F, if using a meat thermometer.

4 Meanwhile, for the whipped corn potatoes, place the potatoes in a large saucepan of cold salted water. Cover and bring to the boil. Lower the heat and cook for about 20 minutes, or until the potatoes are tender. Drain the potatoes and dry them over a low heat. Push the potatoes through a *mouli-légumes* or potato ricer or mash in the traditional way.

5 While the potatoes are cooking, gently warm the olive oil over a medium heat, add the garlic and cook slowly until golden. Remove the garlic from the oil, reserving the oil, and put the garlic in a blender with the double cream and thyme and process until smooth.

(continued opposite)

WHIPPED CORN POTATOES

3 large baking potatoes, peeled and cut into 2.5 cm (1 inch) cubes

150 ml (¼ pint) extra virgin olive oil

5 cloves garlic

300 ml (½ pint) double cream (heavy cream), warmed

2 teaspoons fresh soft thyme leaves

100 g (4 oz) (½ cup) unsalted butter, softened

1 chilli, deseeded and finely diced

4 spring onions (scallions), finely diced

salt and ground white pepper

fresh lemon juice, to taste

kernels from 2 ears of cooked sweetcorn (about 1½ cups corn kernals)

CAB GRAVY

50 g (2 oz) (¼ cup) unsalted butter

4 shallots, finely chopped

1 clove garlic, finely chopped

1 teaspoon fresh soft thyme leaves

1 bay leaf

½ teaspoon ground black pepper

175 ml (6 fl oz) Cabernet Sauvignon red wine

175 ml (6 fl oz) canned beef consommé

salt

6 Little by little, beat the garlic cream mix and the reserved olive oil into the potatoes. Fold in the butter, chilli, spring onions and season to taste. The potatoes should be a loose set. Season with a little lemon juice, to taste, then fold in the sweetcorn and set aside.

7 For the cab gravy, warm half the butter in a pan over a medium heat with the shallots, garlic, thyme and bay leaf. Cook until the shallots are soft but not brown. Add the pepper, porcini soaking liquor and red wine and simmer over a high heat until the liquid has reduced by half. Add the beef consommé and boil to reduce by one-third. Stir in the remaining butter. Season to taste and remove the bay leaf.

8 Let the meatloaf sit for 10 minutes before slicing. Warm through the potatoes, then serve a slice of hot meatloaf on a bed of whipped corn potatoes and a circle of cab gravy.

76 Sausages with Cep Lentils

Good-value cut
Preparation and cooking: 45 minutes, plus soaking time
Serves 4

1 tablespoon olive oil

225 g (8 oz) (9–10 slices) pancetta or smoked streaky bacon, cut into small pieces

1 onion, finely chopped

1 carrot, finely chopped

1 celery stalk, finely diced

1 leek, finely chopped

2 bay leaves

1 teaspoon fresh soft thyme leaves

4 cloves garlic, finely chopped

25 g (1 oz) (½ cup) dried ceps, soaked for 30 minutes in 300 ml (½ pint) boiling water

225 g (8 oz) (1 cup) Puy (French green) lentils, washed

375 ml (13 fl oz) red wine

600 ml (1 pint) beef stock

8 of your favourite beef sausages

50 g (2 oz) (¼ cup) unsalted butter

225 g (8 oz) (4 cups) baby spinach leaves

4 tablespoons fresh flat-leaf parsley, roughly chopped

salt and freshly ground black pepper

I am not a fan of plain beef sausages, but when added to this wonderful lentil casserole they are taken into a different realm. For those of you who are particularly picky, you might want to extract the sausage meat from the skins and create little patties.

1 Heat the olive oil in a heavy-based saucepan. Add the pancetta or bacon and cook over a medium heat until it is golden and has released its natural fats.

2 Add the onion, carrot, celery, leek, bay leaves, thyme and garlic to the pan and cook for 8–10 minutes.

3 Drain the ceps and squeeze dry, retaining the soaking liquor. Chop the ceps finely and add to the cooked vegetables. Stir in the lentils.

4 Strain the cep soaking liquor through muslin or a fine sieve straight into the lentil pan. Add the wine and stock and bring to the boil.

5 Meanwhile, brown the sausages all over in half the butter, cut them into 2.5 cm (1 inch) pieces and pop them into the lentils. Cook for about 30 minutes until the lentils are tender.

6 Fold in the spinach and parsley and cook until wilted. Fold in the remaining butter to enrich and season to taste. Serve piping hot.

77 The Famous Fiorentina T-bone Steak

Prime cut
Preparation and cooking: 45 minutes
Serves 2

2 x T-bone steaks, approximately 2.5 cm (1 inch) thick

85 ml (3 fl oz) extra virgin olive oil

Maldon salt (sea salt) and freshly ground black pepper, to taste

1 lemon, cut into wedges

watercress, to garnish

TOMATO & HERB HOLLANDAISE

see method for ingredients

The Italians usually use chianina beef: top-grade meat reared on certain plains of Italy. They cut their T-bones quite thinly, about 1.5 cm (⅝ inch), but I prefer a steak at least 2.5 cm (1 inch) thick. A classic accompaniment to this steak would be Béarnaise Sauce (see page 125) however here I've chosen something a little different – Tomato and Herb Hollandaise.

1 Remove the steaks from the refrigerator 30 minutes before you want to cook them and coat with the olive oil. Season the steaks with salt and pepper just before cooking. Heat a large griddle pan until it is almost smoking, then drain the steaks of any excess oil.

2 Place them on the griddle pan over a high heat and sear on each side for 2 minutes, then reduce the heat and cook for a further 3 minutes for medium-rare. Amend the cooking time accordingly if you prefer your steaks rare or well-done, and use the 'touch' test described in the introduction (see page 11) to determine when they are ready.

3 Remove the steaks from the pan and leave in a warm place for 5 minutes to settle the meat juices. Serve with the lemon wedges, watercress and Tomato and Herb Hollandaise (see below).

To make the Tomato & Herb Hollandaise
In a saucepan, combine 2 tablespoons each dry white wine and white wine vinegar with 1 finely sliced shallot and ½ teaspoon ground white pepper. Bring to a simmer, reduce until about 1 tablespoon of liquid remains then strain into a liquidizer. Add 1 tablespoon warm water to the liquidizer together with 1 tablespoon tomato purée and two egg yolks and turn on the machine. Pour 250 g (9 oz) (1 cup plus 2 tablespoons) melted hot unsalted butter into a non-drip jug (measuring cup) and start to pour it slowly onto the egg yolks. As the sauce emulsifies, increase the butter flow to a steady slow stream. As it thickens, you will notice a change in the sound of the blender. If the sauce is too thick, add a little more warm water or lemon juice to taste. Add 1 tablespoon each finely chopped basil, chives and parsley plus a pinch of cayenne pepper. Blend briefly and season to taste with salt. Fold in 3 tablespoons diced and seeded tomato. Keep the sauce warm in a bowl or jug set in a pan of hot but not boiling water.

78 Steak Diane

Prime cut
Preparation and cooking: 30 minutes
Serves 2

50 g (2 oz) (¼ cup) unsalted butter

2 x 175 g (6 oz) fillet or sirloin steaks, beaten until 5 mm (¼ inch) thick

salt and freshly ground black pepper

3 shallots, finely diced

2 teaspoons Dijon mustard

1 tablespoon Worcestershire sauce

3 tablespoons red wine

3 tablespoons beef stock

1 tablespoon brandy

3 tablespoons double cream (heavy cream)

1 tablespoon fresh parsley, chopped

Steak Diane was one of those dishes that was always cooked tableside in a restaurant. Unfortunately, not many waiters were particularly good chefs, so the meat was often boiled in the sauce and really tough. This recipe corrects those mistakes.

1 Heat half the butter in a large frying pan. Season the steaks, then cook them over a high heat for 1 minute each side. Remove the steaks from the pan and keep warm.

2 Add the remaining butter to the frying pan with the shallots and cook over a gentle heat for 8 minutes until the shallots have softened.

3 Add the Dijon mustard and Worcestershire sauce to the pan, stir to combine, then add the red wine and stock and bring to the boil. Cook until reduced by one-third, then add the brandy and set light to it. Allow the flames to subside, add the cream and boil over a high heat for about 3 minutes until the sauce is the thickness of single cream (half-and-half cream). Fold in the parsley and season to taste.

4 Return the steaks to the pan and warm through but do not boil. Remove and place the steaks on a plate, top with the sauce and serve with French fries and buttered peas.

79 Sirloin of Beef Topped with Field Mushroom and Taleggio

Prime cut
Preparation and cooking: 50 minutes
Serves 4

8 large field mushrooms

½ tablespoon fresh thyme, roughly chopped

3 tablespoons extra virgin olive oil

juice of 1 lemon

1 large clove garlic, cut into 8 slivers

4 x 250 g (9 oz) sirloin steaks

Maldon salt (sea salt) and freshly ground black pepper

140 g (5 oz) Taleggio cheese (or Bel Paese or fontina), cut into 8 slices

CREAMED SPINACH

1.3 kg (3 lb) fresh-cut spinach, washed and central stalks removed

85 g (3 oz) (¼ cup plus 2 tablespoons) unsalted butter

3 shallots, finely diced

450 ml (16 fl oz) milk

50 g (2 oz) (½ cup) plain flour (all-purpose flour)

¼ teaspoon ground nutmeg

150 ml (¼ pint) double cream (heavy cream)

A wonderful way of jazzing up a good piece of steak. Mushrooms and melting Taleggio cheese are a lovely combination, and you will find creamed spinach is a classic accompaniment to most steaks in America.

1 For the creamed spinach, place the spinach in a large pan of boiling water and cook for 10 minutes. Drain, allow to cool, then squeeze the spinach dry. Chop the spinach and place it in a bowl.

2 Melt the butter in a saucepan and pan-fry the shallots for about 8 minutes until softened but not brown. In a separate pan, heat the milk until small bubbles form on the edges of the pan. Add the flour to the shallots and stir until the mixture is uniform. Stir in the hot milk with the nutmeg, dissolving any lumps. Simmer gently for 20 minutes. Stir the sauce and cream into the chopped spinach, season to taste, and set aside to keep warm.

3 Preheat the oven to 200°C/400°F/Gas Mark 6. Place the mushrooms in a roasting tin (pan). Mix together the thyme, 2 tablespoons olive oil and lemon juice and pour over the mushrooms. Place a slice of garlic on each mushroom and bake them in the oven for 10 minutes.

4 Meanwhile, season the steaks on both sides, rub with the remainder of the olive oil and cook in a griddle pan over a high heat to your liking. Remove from the heat and allow to rest for 2 minutes.

5 Preheat the grill. Remove the mushrooms from the oven and place 2 mushrooms on top of each steak. Place 1 slice of Taleggio over each mushroom and pop the steaks under the grill until the cheese is bubbling and oozing. Serve with the creamed spinach and some sautéed potatoes.

80 Fillet of Beef Stroganoff

Prime cut
Preparation and cooking: 50 minutes
Serves 4

1 tablespoon olive oil

25 g (1 oz) (2 tablespoons) unsalted butter

450 g (1 lb) beef fillet tail, cut into thin strips about 5 x 1 cm (2 x ½ inch)

3 shallots, peeled and finely diced

100 g (4 oz) (1½ cups) button mushrooms, quartered

2 teaspoons tomato purée

1 large sweet and sour gherkin, cut into 5 mm (¼ inch) dice

2 teaspoons smoked paprika

1 teaspoon Dijon mustard

1 teaspoon Worcestershire sauce

4 tablespoons beef stock

1 tablespoon brandy

4 tablespoons soured cream

salt and freshly ground black pepper

2 tablespoons fresh parsley, chopped

A popular dish in the 1960s and 1970s, this has recently made a return to the menu of Notting Grill. An all-time favourite that uses the cheaper cut of fillet; ask your butcher to give you the 'tail'.

1 Heat the oil and butter in a large frying pan. When hot but not quite smoking, add the beef and cook over a high heat, sealing swiftly; it is important that the beef is just seared. Remove the beef from the pan and set aside in a warm place.

2 Add the shallots to the beef pan and cook for 5 minutes over a medium heat. Add the mushrooms and cook for a further 5 minutes. Add the tomato purée, gherkin, paprika, mustard and Worcestershire sauce and stir to combine. Cook for a further 2 minutes.

3 Add the stock and cook over a high heat until the liquid is reduced by half. Return the beef to the pan, add the brandy and set light to it. Allow the flames to subside, then fold in the soured cream. Heat, but do not allow to boil. Season to taste, fold in the parsley and serve with boiled rice and a sprinkling of paprika.

81 Beef Fillet Rossini with Périgueux Sauce

Prime cut
Preparation and cooking: 45 minutes
Serves 4

4 x 175 g (6 oz) beef fillets

175 g (6 oz) duck liver pâté (non force-fed), 100 g (4 oz) cut into 4 slices and the remainder cut into small dice

½ teaspoon chopped truffles

4 thin slices of prosciutto, large enough to wrap around the beef fillets

5 tablespoons vegetable oil

salt and ground black pepper

4 slices truffle

PÉRIGUEUX SAUCE

2 tablespoons truffle juice

4 tablespoons port

4 tablespoons Madeira

400 ml (14 fl oz) beef stock

25 g (1 oz) (2 tablespoons) chopped truffles

40 g (1½ oz) (3 tablespoons) chilled, diced butter

A dish that topped all function menus in the 1950s and 1960s. This is the classic recipe, although I choose not to use *foie gras* as I feel the ducks and geese are treated inhumanely to produce this admittedly delicious gourmet delight.

1 Using a sharp knife, make a horizontal incision in the centre of each beef fillet to form a pocket. Mix the diced duck liver pâté and chopped truffle together and divide between the four pockets. Wrap a slice of prosciutto around each fillet and secure with a cocktail stick or tie with a piece of butcher's string (kitchen twine) to keep the contents in place during cooking.

2 Preheat the oven to 200°C/400°F/Gas Mark 6. Heat the oil in a heavy-based frying pan. Season the beef with the salt and pepper and seal all over in the pan until evenly browned. Transfer to the oven and cook to your taste – about 8 minutes for medium-rare. Ideally, don't cook the beef any more than medium-rare to medium. Remove the beef from the oven and allow it to rest in a warm place.

3 Meanwhile, for the sauce, put the truffle juice, port and Madeira into a small saucepan and reduce to a syrup over a medium heat. Add the beef stock, bring to the boil and reduce until the sauce coats the back of a spoon. Add the chopped truffles, then whisk in the butter, piece by piece, until it is fully incorporated. Remove from the heat and season with salt and ground black pepper.

4 Heat a non-stick pan on the stove until very hot. Season the slices of duck liver pâté lightly with salt and ground black pepper and quickly sear them for 45 seconds on both sides. When both sides are golden, remove the slices from the pan with a spatula. Place a slice of duck liver pâté on top of each piece of beef, and a slice of truffle on the duck liver pâté. Spoon the Périgueux sauce over and around the beef and serve with rösti potato and buttered spinach.

82 Roast Rib of Beef on the Bone with Horseradish Cream

Prime cut
Preparation and cooking: 2 hours 30 minutes, plus marinating time
Serves 6–8

1 teaspoon dried thyme

1 teaspoon dried basil

1/2 teaspoon cayenne pepper

1 teaspoon paprika

1 teaspoon garlic salt

1/2 teaspoon English mustard powder

2.25 kg (5 lb) piece fore-rib (rib-eye) beef, on the bone

2 tablespoons Dijon mustard

3 tablespoons olive oil

1 onion, roughly chopped

1 carrot, roughly chopped

1 leek, roughly chopped

salt and freshly ground black pepper

3 tablespoons dripping (fat from roasted meat) or olive oil

150 ml (1/4 pint) red wine

600 ml (1 pint) fresh beef stock (from a carton is fine, or canned beef consommé)

Horseradish Cream, to serve (for ingredients and method see page 130)

In a recent poll, rib of beef emerged as the nation's favourite roast. Forget topside and choose rib for a really tender, tasty Sunday joint.

1 Place the thyme, basil, cayenne, paprika, garlic salt and mustard powder into a bowl and mix to combine. Wipe the meat with damp kitchen paper (paper towels) and then spread a thin layer of the Dijon mustard all over the fat side of the beef joint. Sprinkle the spice mixture on top, patting it down gently to help it stick. If you have time, wrap loosely in cling film and allow the beef to marinate overnight.

2 Preheat the oven to 200°C/400°F/Gas Mark 6. Pour the 3 tablespoons olive oil into a roasting tin (pan) and allow to heat in the oven for 5 minutes. Add the onion, carrot and leek, tossing to coat them in the oil. Season to taste and roast for 20 minutes until lightly caramelized.

3 Increase the oven temperature to 220°C/425°F/Gas Mark 8. Heat a large, heavy-based frying pan, add the dripping or olive oil and, when the oil is hot, quickly sear the beef for about 30 seconds on each side – be careful as the spices will give off a strong aroma and make your eyes water! Transfer the beef to the roasting tin using the vegetables as a bed to sit it on.

4 Add the red wine to the frying pan and allow to bubble down to burn off the alcohol, then pour into the roasting tin with half of the stock. Roast for 15 minutes until well sealed, then reduce the oven temperature to 200°C/400°F/Gas Mark 6 once again and roast for 10 minutes per 450 g (1 lb) for rare; 12 minutes per 450 g (1 lb) for medium-rare; or 20–25 minutes per 450 g (1 lb) for well done. Baste the roast with the red wine and stock every 10 minutes or so during cooking.

5 Remove the beef from the tin and place on a large dish. Allow to rest in a warm place for at least 10–15 minutes before carving. To make the gravy, pour the remaining stock into the roasting tin and place directly on the hob (stovetop) to heat. Cook for 5 minutes, stirring and scraping the bottom with a wooden spoon to remove any sediment. Season and pour through a sieve into a gravy boat. Carve the beef into slices and arrange on serving plates with vegetables, roast potatoes, Yorkshire puddings and the Horseradish Cream (see page 130). Hand the gravy around separately.

83 Hunter Steak

Prime cut
Preparation and cooking: 1 hour, plus marinating time
Serves 6

4 x 225 g (8 oz) sirloin steaks, 1–2.5 cm ($\frac{1}{2}$–1 inch) thick

600 ml (1 pint) gutsy red wine

125 ml (4 fl oz) each port and Madeira

30 ml (1 fl oz) brandy

10 cloves garlic

3 onions, roughly chopped

1 celery stalk, finely sliced

2 shallots, sliced

1 carrot, peeled and chopped

1 teaspoon soft thyme leaves

1 bay leaf, crushed

1$\frac{1}{2}$ teaspoons dried basil

$\frac{1}{2}$ teaspoon dried marjoram

12 juniper berries, roasted

2 tablespoons fresh parsley stems, plus 2 tablespoons fresh parsley, chopped, to serve

100 g (4 oz) ($\frac{1}{2}$ cup) butter

85 g (3 oz) extra-lean minced (ground) beef

600 ml (1 pint) beef stock

$\frac{1}{4}$ of a celeriac, peeled

3 plum tomatoes, peeled

3 tablespoons cooked tongue

85 g (3 oz) (1$\frac{1}{4}$ cups) button mushrooms, finely sliced

salt and ground black pepper

This is a dish that requires the steak to be marinated and accompanied by a wonderful sauce that requires a few cheffy skills but is well worth the effort. Allow for 3 days' marinating time.

1 Trim the steaks of all fat and gristle. Keep any trimmings of meat you can find from the 'chain', which is very little, and chop finely. Place the steaks in a large glass baking dish.

2 Put the red wine, port, Madeira and brandy into a pan and bring to the boil. Crush the garlic to a paste with a little salt. Add this and the onions, celery, shallots, carrot, thyme, crushed bay leaf, basil, marjoram, juniper berries (crushed) and the chopped parsley stems, simmer together for 15 minutes, then cool completely. Pour the marinade over the steaks and marinate for 3 days, turning once a day.

3 On the fourth day, heat 15 g ($\frac{1}{2}$ oz) (1 tablespoon) of the butter in a pan over a medium heat and brown the beef mince along with the chopped steak trimmings. Retrieve and pat dry the vegetables from the marinade. Toss them with the beef mince until dry and starting to brown. Mix the liquid marinade with the beef stock, then gradually add it to the meat and vegetables, 75 ml (2$\frac{1}{2}$ fl oz) at a time, and reducing by half each time. There should be 300 ml ($\frac{1}{2}$ pint) of stock by the time you have finished. Strain into a small saucepan, bring to the boil, add 65 g (2$\frac{1}{2}$ oz) (5 tablespoons) of the butter and boil until emulsified.

4 Heat the remaining butter in a frying pan and pan-fry the steaks to your liking. Discard the cooking butter, add the sauce and stir to remove any meat bits from the bottom of the pan.

5 Cut the celeriac into 3 mm ($\frac{1}{8}$ inch) matchsticks and blanch briefly in a pan of boiling water. Deseed the plum tomatoes and cut into 5 mm ($\frac{1}{4}$ inch) dice. Now cut the cooked tongue into 3 mm ($\frac{1}{8}$ inch) matchsticks. Add all of these plus the mushrooms, season to taste and cook until the vegetables are tender. Serve the steaks topped with the sauce and chopped parsley.

84 Classic Steak au Poivre

Prime cut
Preparation and cooking: 30 minutes
Serves 2

450 g (1 lb) piece rump or sirloin steak, about 5 cm (2 inches) thick

3 teaspoons black peppercorns, crushed

Maldon salt (sea salt)

25 g (1 oz) (2 tablespoons) unsalted butter

1 tablespoon olive oil

2 tablespoons brandy

2 teaspoons Dijon mustard

1 teaspoon Worcestershire sauce

6 tablespoons beef stock

2 tablespoons gutsy red wine

1 tablespoon green peppercorns in brine, drained

6 tablespoons double cream (heavy cream)

One of the biggest sellers at Notting Grill, this 1960s classic will always be popular. Some people add cream, some don't; the choice must be yours, but for me it works better with cream.

1 Preheat the oven to 190°C/375°F/Gas Mark 5.

2 Press the crushed peppercorns into both sides of the steak and sprinkle with salt. Heat the butter and oil in a heavy-based, ovenproof frying pan over a high heat, and when foaming add the steak. Cook for 2 minutes on each side. Pop in to the preheated oven and cook for a further 8 minutes if you like your meat medium-rare, or to your liking. Remove from the oven, transfer the steak to a plate and set aside in a warm place to rest.

3 Over a medium heat, add the brandy to the pan, scraping the meat juices from the bottom of the pan, then add the mustard, Worcestershire sauce, stock and red wine. Whisk to combine, and cook until the sauce has reduced by one-third. Pour into the sauce any juices that have seeped from the beef. Add the green peppercorns and cream and cook for a further 2 minutes. Season to taste with salt.

4 Slice the rested steak on the diagonal, then arrange the slices on 2 plates and pour over the pepper sauce. Serve with a leaf salad, some buttered leaf spinach and new Jersey potatoes (or any new potato variety).

85 Spice-and-Salt-Cured Beef

Prime cut
Preparation and cooking: 40 minutes, plus marinating time
Serves 6–8

3 tablespoons brown sugar

2 teaspoons fresh thyme leaves, chopped

2 cloves garlic, crushed to a paste with a little salt

¼ teaspoon ground cloves

½ teaspoon ground ginger

½ teaspoon ground allspice

½ teaspoon nutmeg, freshly grated

2 tablespoons freshly ground black pepper

1 teaspoon ground coriander seeds

1 x 1.5 kg (3 lb 5 oz) beef fillet, centre-cut

3 tablespoons Maldon salt (sea salt)

1 tablespoon olive oil

This dish needs some advanced preparation but is a lovely thing to serve at a buffet, party or over the Christmas period. Allow for 10 days' marinating time.

1 In a small bowl, stir together the sugar, thyme, garlic, cloves, ginger, allspice, nutmeg, pepper and coriander seeds. Rub the beef fillet with the spice mixture and place it an ovenproof dish. Cover with cling film and refrigerate for 2 days, turning from time to time.

2 After 2 days, rub the fillet with the salt and refrigerate for a further 8 days, turning the meat once a day.

3 Preheat the oven to 180°C/350°F/Gas Mark 4. Heat the oil in a large griddle pan and sear the beef all over until brown. Place the beef in the oven and cook for 15–30 minutes, depending on how you like it cooked. Serve in slices with the traditional accompaniments for roast beef.

86 Beef Wellington

Prime cut
Preparation and cooking: 1 hour
Serves 6–8

a little olive oil

15 g (½ oz) (1 tablespoon) unsalted butter

1.5 kg (3 lb) piece beef fillet, centre-cut

salt and freshly ground black pepper

375 g (13 oz) ready-rolled puff pastry, thawed if frozen

plain flour (all-purpose flour), for dusting

4 ready-made pancakes (crêpes)

175 g (6 oz) chicken liver pâté

1 small egg, beaten

MUSHROOM STUFFING

50 g (2 oz) (¼ cup) unsalted butter

140 g (5 oz) (¾ cup) shallots, finely diced

250 g (9 oz) (1¾ cups) flat mushrooms, finely chopped

3 tablespoons double cream (heavy cream)

How often are you served Beef Wellington and wonder how to make it? Well, here's the answer. This is a classic dish that keeps the cost of fillet steak to a minimum.

1 Heat the olive oil and the butter in a non-stick frying pan. Season the beef. When the pan is hot, add the beef and quickly seal all over. Remove from the pan, place on a plate and allow to cool completely.

2 For the mushroom stuffing, heat the butter in the frying pan until hot and foaming. Add the shallots and cook until softened and lightly golden. Add the mushrooms and cook gently, stirring until all the liquid evaporates. Add the cream to the pan and season generously. Continue to heat gently until the mixture has reduced to a thick purée. Set aside to cool completely.

3 Preheat the oven to 230°C/450°F/Gas Mark 8. Roll out the pastry on a lightly floured work surface to fit the beef comfortably and lay two of the pancakes on top, slightly overlapping. Spread a strip of chicken liver pâté across the centre of the pancakes, to the same width as the beef fillet.

4 Make a lengthways cut into the centre of the beef about three-quarters of the way through and fill with the cooled mushroom stuffing. Place the beef on the pancakes and cover with the remaining two pancakes, slightly overlapping. Cut away the middle of the ends of the pastry. Fold the long edges of the pastry over the meat and then neatly fold in the ends, dampening the edges to seal.

5 Place the wrapped beef fillet seam-side down on a large, non-stick baking sheet (cookie sheet). Decorate the top with the pastry trimmings if desired, and brush all over with the beaten egg. Place in the oven for 10 minutes, then reduce the heat to 190°C/375°F/Gas Mark 5 and continue to cook for another 20 minutes until the pastry is puffed up and golden brown. Remove from the oven to a carving board and allow to rest for 5 minutes before carving into thick slices. Serve at once with steamed purple sprouting broccoli and new potatoes.

87 Chateaubriand with Béarnaise Sauce

Prime cut
Preparation and cooking: 30 minutes
Serves 4

1 x thick end of a whole fillet (about 700 g/1 lb 9 oz), called the chateaubriand

1 tablespoon olive oil

½ teaspoon Maldon salt (sea salt)

¼ teaspoon fresh ground black pepper

BÉARNAISE SAUCE

2 tablespoons dry white wine

2 tablespoons tarragon vinegar

2 tablespoons fresh tarragon leaves, finely chopped

1 shallot, finely sliced

½ teaspoon ground white pepper

warm water

2 egg yolks

250 g (9 oz) (1 cup plus 2 tablespoons) unsalted butter, melted and hot

lemon juice, to taste

1 tablespoon fresh parsley, finely chopped

pinch cayenne pepper

This is a traditional way of using this cut, which is taken from the thick end of the fillet. I have given you my quick version of Béarnaise sauce, which takes all the hassle out of what can be a tricky little number.

1 Allow the chateaubriand to come to room temperature before cooking. Rub all over with the olive oil, then sprinkle with the salt and pepper. Preheat the oven to its hottest setting: 240°C/475°F/Gas Mark 9.

2 Heat a heavy-based ovenproof frying pan. Seal the chateaubriand on all sides until golden brown – about 6 minutes over a high heat. Transfer the pan to the oven and roast the steak for about 12 minutes for medium-rare, or to your liking. Remove from the oven and allow to rest in a warm place for 10 minutes.

3 Meanwhile, prepare the Béarnaise sauce. Combine the white wine, vinegar, 1 tablespoon tarragon leaves, shallot and pepper in a saucepan. Bring to a simmer and reduce until about 1 tablespoon of liquid remains. Strain into a liquidizer, pushing down on the tarragon leaves to extract the liquid.

4 Add 1 tablespoon warm water to the liquidizer together with the egg yolks and turn on the machine. Pour the hot butter into a non-drip jug (measuring cup) and start to pour the butter slowly onto the egg yolks. As the sauce emulsifies, increase the butter flow to a steady slow stream. As the sauce thickens, you will notice a change in the sound of the blender. If the sauce is too thick, add a little more warm water or lemon juice to taste. Add the remaining tarragon leaves, the parsley and cayenne pepper and blend briefly. Season to taste with salt. Keep the sauce warm in a bowl or jug set in a pan of hot but not boiling water.

5 Carve the chateaubriand into 12 slices, divide between 4 warm plates, and serve with watercress and Béarnaise sauce on the side and a big bowl of chips (French fries).

88 Boeuf Bourguignonne

Good-value cut
Preparation and cooking: 4 hours, plus marinating time
Serves 6–8

4 tablespoons olive oil

1 large carrot, cut into chunks

1 large onion, cut into chunks

2 celery stalks, roughly chopped

2 bottles red Burgundy wine

2 sprigs of fresh thyme

1 head (bulb) garlic, cut in half horizontally

4 fresh bay leaves

1.3 kg (3 lb) chuck or blade beef steak, cut into 5 cm (2 inch) cubes

50 g (2 oz) ($\frac{1}{4}$ cup) unsalted butter

225 g (8 oz) pancetta, cut into lardons (or 9–10 slices smoked streaky bacon, cut into small strips)

450 g (1 lb) shallots, peeled

2 tablespoons plain flour (all-purpose flour)

300 ml ($\frac{1}{2}$ pint) fresh beef stock (from a carton is fine, or canned beef consommé)

salt and freshly ground black pepper

350 g (12 oz) ($4\frac{1}{2}$ cups) small chestnut mushrooms, trimmed

5 tablespoons brandy

fresh flat-leaf parsley, chopped, to garnish

An all-time classic that provides the perfect marriage of beef and wine in a delicious dish served with creamy buttery mash.

1 Heat 1 tablespoon of the oil in a large pan. Add the carrot, onion and celery and cook for 2–3 minutes, stirring occasionally. Pour in the wine and stir in the thyme, garlic and two of the bay leaves. Bring to the boil, then reduce the heat and simmer for 15 minutes. Allow to cool completely.

2 Place the beef in a large, non-metallic bowl and pour over the wine mixture. Cover with cling film and place in the fridge overnight to marinate. Preheat the oven to 150°C/300°F/Gas Mark 2. Strain the beef into a colander set over a bowl. Reserve the marinade and set aside.

3 Heat 25 g (1 oz) (2 tablespoons) of the butter and 1 tablespoon of the oil in a large frying pan. Add the bacon and cook until sizzling and golden brown, stirring occasionally. Stir in the shallots then transfer to a large casserole dish. Heat another tablespoon of the oil in the frying pan. Pat dry the drained beef cubes with kitchen paper (paper towels). Add half of the beef to the pan and cook until browned on all sides.

4 Remove the beef from the pan with a slotted spoon and add to the bacon and shallot mixture in the casserole dish. Repeat with the remaining beef. Add 2–3 large spoonfuls of the reserved marinade mixture to the frying pan and allow to bubble down, scraping the bottom of the pan with a wooden spoon to remove any sediment. Pour into the casserole dish.

5 Sprinkle the flour into the casserole dish and then add the remaining marinade mixture, bay leaves and the beef stock, stirring to combine. Season generously and bring to the boil, then cover and place in the oven for 3–3$\frac{1}{2}$ hours until the beef is very tender but still holding its shape.

6 Halfway through cooking, heat the remaining oil and butter in a large frying pan and cook the mushrooms until just tender and lightly browned, stirring. Add the brandy and cook for another few minutes, then stir into the casserole dish and return to the oven for the remaining cooking time. Remove from the oven, season to taste, sprinkle with the parsley and serve.

89 Poached Fillet of Beef in Cep Broth with Spring Vegetables

Prime cut
Preparation and cooking: 3 hours 50 minutes
Serves 8

50 g (2 oz) (1 cup) best-quality dried ceps, soaked in warm water for at least 1 hour

**16 each:
baby leeks, asparagus tips, baby turnips, baby carrots, baby new potatoes, sugar snap (snow or mangetout) peas, green haricot (French) beans**

2 tablespoons olive oil

1.8 kg (4 lb) fillet of beef, fat removed and tied

salt and ground black pepper

POACHING LIQUOR

½ bunch celery, washed

1 head (bulb) garlic

1 lb (450 g) tomatoes, peeled, quartered and deseeded

½ savoy cabbage, washed

1 lb (450 g) leeks, washed

225 g (8 oz) each carrots and turnips, peeled

1 onion, peeled and stuck with 2 bay leaves and 2 cloves

3 sprigs fresh thyme

½ bunch fresh chervil

1 tablespoon Maldon Salt (sea salt)

12 white peppercorns

2.8 litres (5 pints) beef stock

Why doesn't anyone think of poaching beef? This dish is delicious, and the beef is rendered very tender with lots of flavour – perfect.

1 For the poaching liquor, cut the celery vertically in two and cut the garlic horizontally in half. Leave the rest of the vegetables whole (unless otherwise instructed). Put these and the rest of the poaching liquor ingredients into a large pan and simmer very gently for 2 hours. Strain and discard the vegetables, herbs and spices. Pour the liquid back into a clean saucepan and return to the heat.

2 Meanwhile, remove the ceps from the water, squeeze out the juices, then strain the juices into the stock. Rinse the ceps under cold water to remove any grit and add to the stock. Simmer for a further hour, topping up with water if necessary.

3 During this hour, begin preparing the vegetables. Bring a pan of salted water to the boil and cook each vegetable – leeks (left whole), asparagus, turnips (scraped, leaving 2.5 cm (1 inch) of green top), carrots (scraped, leaving 2.5 cm (1 inch) of green top), potatoes (scraped, left whole), sugar snap peas and haricot beans – separately, removing when cooked and plunging into iced cold water.

4 Heat the oil in a large frying pan, season the beef and seal all over until golden brown, then place the meat into the simmering stock. Cook for 8–10 minutes per pound for a wonderfully rosy interior. When the meat is cooked to your liking, remove and set aside to rest for 10 minutes, retaining the stock. Meanwhile, make the Anchoïade Rémoulade Sauce (see below).

5 Just before serving, add the vegetables to the broth to reheat. Place the meat on a large platter surrounded by the vegetables and a little broth. Serve with the Anchoïade Rémoulade Sauce, Salsa Verde (see page 131) and Dijon mustard.

To make the Anchoïade Rémoulade Sauce
Blend 2 egg yolks, 1 teaspoon Dijon mustard, 2 tablespoons torn fresh basil, 8 rinsed anchovy fillets and 25 g (1 oz) (3 tablespoons) rinsed capers together in a food processor until smooth. With the machine running, add 425 ml (¾ pint) extra virgin olive oil, little by little, then add 3 tablespoons freshly squeezed lemon juice and plenty of freshly ground black pepper. Garnish with 1 tablespoon each chopped capers and chopped gherkins, and some ripped basil.

90 David's Café de Paris Butter

Preparation: 10 minutes, plus resting time
Makes 500 g (1 lb 2 oz)

450g (1 lb) (2 cups) butter, cubed, at room temperature

2½ tablespoons tomato ketchup

1½ tablespoons English mustard

25 g (1 oz) (3 tablespoons) capers

2 shallots, finely chopped

1 handful fresh parsley, finely chopped

1 tablespoon fresh chives, snipped

½ teaspoon each fresh thyme and fresh chopped marjoram

6 fresh tarragon leaves, finely chopped

½ teaspoon fresh rosemary, chopped

1 clove garlic, finely chopped

6 anchovy fillets, finely chopped

1 tablespoon each brandy and Madeira

½ teaspoon Worcestershire sauce

1 tablespoon paprika

½ teaspoon each curry powder and cayenne

juice and grated zest of 1 unwaxed lemon

grated zest of 1 orange

1 teaspoon salt

David Wilby is the Operations Director for all three of my restaurants. Unlike myself, he is a man with classical training, and the Café de Paris Butter is a classical accompaniment to any type of steak. It may seem like an awful lot of work, but I promise you it is well worth the effort.

1 Soften the butter and beat until fluffy.

2 Combine all the remaining ingredients together and set aside for 4 hours.

3 Combine the butter with the rest of the ingredients, then transfer the butter to a sheet of cling film and roll into a log roughly 2.5 cm (1 inch) in diameter. Refrigerate or freeze until ready to use.

91 Tomato-Green Peppercorn Butter

Preparation: 10 minutes
Makes approximately 250 g (9 oz)

2 tablespoons fresh parsley, stalks removed

2 cloves garlic

4 sun-dried tomatoes, drained

2 teaspoons fresh rosemary

1 tablespoon green peppercorns in brine, drained

1 tablespoon lemon juice

½ teaspoon Maldon salt (sea salt)

250 g (9 oz) (1 cup plus 2 tablespoons) unsalted butter, at room temperature

A great butter to serve with any prime cut of beef – or simply spread on hot toast!

1 Blanch the parsley leaves for 2 minutes in boiling water, then drain. Finely chop the garlic cloves, sun-dried tomatoes and very finely chop the rosemary.

2 In a food processor, pulse together the parsley, garlic, tomatoes, rosemary, peppercorns, lemon juice and salt until roughly blended. Add the butter and pulse until combined.

3 Transfer the butter to a sheet of cling film and roll into a log roughly 2.5 cm (1 inch) in diameter. Refrigerate or freeze until ready to use.

92 Horseradish Cream

Preparation: 10 minutes
Makes about 200 ml (7 fl oz)

5 cm (2 inch) piece fresh horseradish root

85 ml (3 fl oz) soured cream

50 ml (2 fl oz) mayonnaise (home-made or from a jar)

1 tablespoon Dijon mustard

1½ teaspoons fresh lemon juice

pinch caster (fine granulated or berry) sugar

salt and ground black pepper

This is a great accompaniment to your Sunday Roast. If you can't find fresh horseradish root, simply follow the recipe using 3 tablespoons of ready-grated horseradish, which you can buy in jars from most major supermarkets.

1 Peel and finely grate the horseradish root. Place the cream in a bowl and whisk until lightly whipped.

2 Add the horseradish, mayonnaise, mustard, lemon juice and sugar to the cream. Season to taste and stir until well blended. Spoon into a serving bowl and chill until ready to serve.

93 Salsa Verde

Preparation: 10 minutes
Makes 250 ml (8 fl oz)

2 handfuls fresh flat-leaf parsley

12 fresh basil leaves

1 small handful fresh mint leaves

2 pickled cucumbers or large gherkins

3 garlic cloves

2 tablespoons capers, rinsed

4 anchovy fillets, rinsed

1 tablespoon red wine vinegar

1 tablespoon lemon juice

6 tablespoons extra virgin olive oil

1 tablespoon Dijon mustard

$\frac{1}{2}$ teaspoon Maldon salt (sea salt)

$\frac{1}{4}$ teaspoon freshly ground black pepper

A great Italian sauce, excellent served with grilled meats or boiled beef dishes. It's at its best when freshly made, and if you can afford the time, hand-chopping produces a more authentic result than using a food processor. Try it with fish too – delicious.

1 Coarsely chop the herbs, cucumbers or gherkins, garlic, capers and anchovies by hand, or pulse in a food processor.

2 Transfer the mixture to a non-metallic bowl and gradually whisk in the vinegar, lemon juice, olive oil, mustard, salt and pepper. Set aside, covered with cling film, at room temperature until ready to use.

94 Salsa Verde Butter

Preparation: 15 minutes
Makes approximately 400 g (14 oz)

12 spinach leaves

1 bunch watercress leaves

1 tablespoon fresh tarragon leaves

4 tablespoons fresh parsley leaves

4 tablespoons fresh chervil leaves

4 shallots, peeled and chopped

4 baby gherkins, rinsed and chopped

6 anchovy fillets

3 tablespoons capers, rinsed, soaked for 2 hours, then drained

2 cloves garlic

½ teaspoon cayenne pepper

salt and freshly ground black pepper

5 hard-boiled (hard-cooked) egg yolks

2 large raw egg yolks

250 g (9 oz) (1 cup plus 2 tablespoons) unsalted butter, at room temperature

125 ml (4 fl oz) extra virgin olive oil

2 teaspoons white wine vinegar

If you enjoy Salsa Verde, keep a roll of this butter in the fridge or freezer, ready to pop a slice onto your steaks. I've used rib-eye steak here but this butter is excellent with any prime cut of beef. To find out how to cook steak to your liking, follow my advice on pages 10 and 11.

1 Blanch the spinach, watercress, herbs and shallots in boiling water for 1 minute, then drain, refresh under cold water and squeeze dry.

2 Put the spinach mixture in a food processor. Add the baby gherkins, anchovies, capers, garlic, cayenne pepper and seasoning. Process to a smooth paste.

3 Add the egg yolks and the butter and process again until thoroughly mixed. Add the oil, little by little, until the mixture is smooth and glossy. Beat in the vinegar and add salt and pepper to taste. Transfer the butter to a sheet of cling film and roll into a log roughly 2.5 cm (1 inch) in diameter. Refrigerate or freeze until ready to use.

95 Anchovy Butter

| Preparation: 15 minutes |
| Makes approximately 300 g (10 oz) |

12 anchovy fillets

1 tablespoon fresh chives, snipped

2 teaspoons Dijon mustard

2 tablespoons fresh basil, chopped

25 g (1 oz) (3 tablespoons) capers

juice and grated zest of 1 unwaxed lemon

1/2 teaspoon ground black pepper

1 sweet-and-sour pickled cucumber, roughly chopped

250 g (9 oz) (1 cup plus 2 tablespoons) unsalted butter, cut into smallish cubes, at room temperature

The ideal replacement for salt, this butter goes perfectly with grilled steak.

1 Roughly chop the anchovy fillets with 1 tablespoon of their oil.

2 In a food processor, pulse together the chopped anchovies, chives, mustard, basil, capers, lemon juice and zest, pepper and cucumber until roughly blended. With the machine running, add the butter piece by piece until thoroughly combined, scraping down the sides of the container from time to time.

3 Transfer the butter to a sheet of cling film and roll into a log roughly 2.5 cm (1 inch) in diameter. Refrigerate or freeze until ready to use.

96 Italian Bread Sauce

| Preparation and cooking: 30 minutes |
| Serves 4–6 |

4 x 10 cm (4 inch) bone marrow shafts, soaked in iced water

300 ml (1/2 pint) beef stock

6 tablespoons red wine

2 thick slices white country bread, crusts removed, crumbled

2 tablespoons fresh Parmesan cheese, grated

salt and ground black pepper

Although I love English bread sauce, I feel this wins hands down. It's a lovely accompaniment to poultry as well as grilled beef. You have to try it!

1 Push the bone marrow out of the bones and chop finely.

2 Put the stock and wine into a small saucepan, add the bread and cook over a low heat until the bread emulsifies with the liquid.

3 Fold in the cheese and the bone marrow and continue to cook until both have melted into the sauce. Season with salt and pepper. Keep warm until ready to use.

97 Garlic Steak Condiment

Preparation: 40 minutes
Makes approximately 300 ml (½ pint)

1 head (bulb) garlic

150 ml (¼ pint) tomato ketchup

75 ml (2½ fl oz) Worcestershire sauce

1 onion, finely diced

2 teaspoons Tabasco sauce

1 tablespoon sweet paprika

1 tablespoon Colman's dry mustard powder

75 ml (2½ fl oz) organic cider vinegar

salt and ground black pepper

A perfect sauce in which to marinate your steak, or simply sprinkle on top after cooking.

1 Roast the head of garlic for 30 minutes and then push each clove out of its skin. Put the cloves and all the rest of the ingredients in a saucepan and mix to combine. Place over a low heat and cook gently for 20 minutes. Allow the mixture to cool, then blend in a liquidizer, pass through a fine sieve, and bottle. Keeps for at least 1 month.

2 For a warm sauce, heat the condiment in a pan and add 125 g (4½ oz) (½ cup) cold cubes of unsalted butter, piece by piece, whisking constantly. Season to taste.

98 Burger or Steak Seasoning Salt

Preparation: 5 minutes
Makes approximately 250 g (9 oz)

225 g (8 oz) (1 cup) Maldon salt (sea salt)

1 tablespoon dried oregano

2 tablespoons ground black pepper

1 teaspoon bay powder or ground dried bay leaves (use a spice- or coffee-grinder to grind the leaves)

½ tablespoon each onion powder, garlic powder, dried thyme, cayenne pepper, smoked paprika

If you are making your own burgers, add a little of this to your mix or sprinkle on a burger or steak just prior to cooking.

1 Combine all the ingredients; place in a spice- or coffee-grinder and grind to a fine powder.

2 Store in a glass jar and sprinkle on your burger or steak just prior to cooking.

99 Roasted Onion and Garlic Sauce

<table>
<tr><td>Preparation and cooking:
1 hour 30 minutes</td></tr>
<tr><td>Serves 2–4</td></tr>
</table>

1 Spanish onion, peeled and cut into 12 wedges

1 tablespoon olive oil

1 head (bulb) garlic, broken into cloves but not peeled

½ teaspoon Maldon salt (sea salt)

½ teaspoon freshly ground black pepper

½ teaspoon fresh thyme leaves

300 ml (½ pint) beef stock

1 teaspoon soy sauce

A really excellent sauce to accompany all sorts of grilled meats (I've used sirloin steak here), and involving two of my favourite flavours: onion and garlic. It's easy to overcook steak so, if you like it more rare, follow my tips and advice on pages 10 and 11.

1 Preheat the oven to 160°C/325°F/Gas Mark 3. Place the onion wedges in a small roasting pan with the olive oil and toss to combine. Place in the oven and cook for 30 minutes.

2 After 30 minutes add the garlic, salt, pepper and thyme leaves and mix well to coat with the oil. Cook for a further 30 minutes. Allow to cool slightly before squeezing each clove of garlic out of its skin. Place the garlic in a blender with the onion and thyme.

3 Pour the beef stock into the roasting pan with the soy sauce and stir to combine with any meat juices from your roasted or pan-fried steak or joint, salt and pepper. Pour into the blender with the garlic mixture, switch on the machine and blend until smooth. Pass the sauce through a fine sieve and reheat when ready to serve.

100 Pinot Noir Butter Sauce

Preparation and cooking: 30 minutes
Serves 2–4

1 tablespoon olive oil

4 shallots, finely diced

1 clove garlic, finely chopped

1 teaspoon fresh soft thyme leaves

175 ml (6 fl oz) Pinot Noir red wine

175 ml (6 fl oz) beef stock

125 g (4½ oz) (½ cup) unsalted butter, very cold and cut into small cubes

salt and freshly ground black pepper

1 teaspoon red wine vinegar

I'm not a classically trained chef, but there are times when you have to agree that some classic recipes justifiedly retain their popularity. This is one of them. You could make this to go with any type of steak; here, I've opted for tender fillet. By following my simple instructions on pages 10 and 11 you will be able to cook your steak as rare or as well done as you like.

1 Heat the olive oil in a pan over a medium heat, then add the shallots, garlic and thyme. Allow to cook slowly until soft but not too coloured.

2 Pour in the wine and stock, increase the heat and boil until the liquid is reduced by half.

3 Add 2 pieces of butter at a time, whisking continuously; work on and off the heat so the butter emulsifies with the sauce. When the butter is fully incorporated, season to taste with salt, pepper and vinegar. Keep the sauce warm but do not place over a direct heat.

Chilli-peanut Sauce

4 spring onions (scallions)

2 fresh red chillies

1 tablespoon groundnut
(peanut) oil

1 teaspoon each fresh ginger and
lemongrass, finely chopped

5 cloves garlic, chopped

1 teaspoon dried chilli flakes

300 ml ($\frac{1}{2}$ pint) chicken stock

1 tablespoon each soy sauce,
Tamarind paste and lime juice

300 ml ($\frac{1}{2}$ pint) coconut milk

$\frac{1}{2}$ teaspoon cumin powder

350 g (12 oz) ($1\frac{1}{3}$ cups) crunchy
peanut butter

140 g (5 oz) ($1\frac{1}{2}$ cups) soft
brown sugar

salt, to taste

1 Finely chop the spring onions and red chillies. Heat the oil in a pan over a medium heat, then pan-fry the onions, chillies, ginger, lemongrass, garlic and dried chillies for 4–5 minutes until the onions have softened without colouring.

2 Add the chicken stock and bring to the boil. Reduce the heat, add the remaining ingredients and simmer the sauce for 10–15 minutes, uncovered, until thickened. The oil may separate but just give it a stir to re-emulsify. If necessary, add a little extra stock if the sauce is too thick. Remove from the heat and allow to cool. Spoon into a clean jar and refrigerate until ready to use.

Jewelled Couscous

85 g (3 oz) ($\frac{1}{2}$ cup) dried apricots

400 ml (14 fl oz) chicken or
vegetable stock

2 tablespoons extra virgin olive oil

1 teaspoon salt

225 g (8 oz) ($1\frac{1}{4}$ cups) couscous

finely grated rind of 1 lemon and
juice of $\frac{1}{2}$ lemon (unwaxed)

50 g (2 oz) ($\frac{1}{2}$ cup) toasted
flaked almonds

50 g (2 oz) ($\frac{1}{3}$ cup) sultanas
(golden raisins) or raisins

6 tablespoons fresh flat-leaf
parsley, roughly chopped

6 tablespoons fresh coriander
leaves (cilantro), roughly
chopped

salt and freshly ground black
pepper

1 Soak the dried apricots in a little water for 20 minutes, then drain and chop. Heat the stock in a large pan with 1 tablespoon of the olive oil and the salt. Bring to a simmer, remove from the heat and pour in the couscous in a thin, steady stream. Stir in the lemon rind and juice. Set aside for 2 minutes to allow the grains to swell – they should soak up all of the liquid.

2 Return the couscous to the heat and drizzle over the remaining olive oil. Heat gently for about 5 minutes, stirring with a long-pronged fork to fluff up the grains, then remove from the heat. Fold in the apricots, almonds, sultanas or raisins, parsley and coriander, and season to taste.

Curry Paste

1 tablespoon each coriander seeds and cumin seeds

1/2 teaspoon black peppercorns

1/2 teaspoon ground nutmeg

1/4 teaspoon ground cloves

3 green cardamom pods

2 strips dried orange peel (optional), ground to a powder

1 tablespoon groundnut (peanut) or vegetable oil

3 spring onions (scallions), roughly chopped

2 hot red chillies, coarsely chopped

4 cloves garlic

1 lemongrass stalk, outside leaves removed, bruised and finely sliced

2 teaspoons *blachan* (shrimp paste)

2 tablespoons fresh coriander leaves (cilantro)

2 tablespoons water

1 Dry-roast the coriander seeds, cumin seeds and black peppercorns in a hot frying pan until fragrant. Crush the toasted spices in a pestle and mortar or in an electric spice- or coffee-grinder. Combine with the nutmeg, cloves, cardamom and orange peel, if using. Set aside.

2 Meanwhile, heat the oil in a frying pan and add the onions, chillies, garlic and lemongrass. Pan-fry over a high heat until lightly charred, then fold in the shrimp paste and stir to combine. Cook gently for a further 2 minutes.

3 Place the spice mix, the onion mix, the coriander leaves and water in a food processor and blend until smooth, adding extra water if necessary. Set aside until ready to cook the curry.

Rustic Tomato Sauce

3 tablespoons extra virgin olive oil

1/2 onion, finely chopped

1 garlic clove, finely chopped

1 teaspoon fresh soft thyme leaves

125 ml (4 fl oz) dry white wine

1 x 400 g (14 oz) can chopped tomatoes

4 tablespoons mixed fresh herbs (flat-leaf parsley, chives, oregano), coarsely chopped

salt and freshly ground black pepper

1 Heat the olive oil in a large saucepan, then add the onion, garlic and thyme leaves and cook over a medium heat for about 8 minutes, until the onion has softened but not browned.

2 Add the white wine, then increase the heat, add the tomatoes and cook for a further 12 minutes until the liquid has reduced and you have a fairly thick sauce. Add the chopped herbs and season to taste.

Index

Food photography by Steve Lee

Published by BBC Books, BBC Worldwide Ltd,
80 Wood Lane, London W12 0TT
First published 2005

© Antony Worrall Thompson 2005
The moral right of the author has been asserted
Food photography © BBC Worldwide 2005
Author photographs (cover and p 6) © Robin
Matthews 2005
Beef cut photography (p 8) © Meat and
Livestock Commission 2005
Beef illustration (p 9) by Ann Ramsbottom
© BBC Worldwide 2005
The Publishers would like to thank the Meat and
Livestock Commission for the use of the beef
pictures on p 8.

ISBN 0 563 48785 2

Commissioning Editor: Vivien Bowler
Project Editor: Dee O'Reilly
Copy-editor: Rachel Connolly
Cover Art Director: Pene Parker
Book Designer: Lisa Pettibone
Food Stylist: Clare Greenstreet
Stylist: Jo Harris
Production Controller: Arlene Alexander

Set in Caecilia and Foundry Sans
Printed and bound in France by Imprimerie
Pollina : L95296
Colour separations by Butler & Tanner
Origination

I'd like to thank Jacinta, my wife; Louise, my PA;
Steve for his photography and Dee, my Project
Editor at BBC Books, all of whom helped to bring
this book to fruition.

If you require further information on any BBC
Worldwide product call 08700 777 001 or visit
our website on www.bbcshop.com

If you would like further information about
Antony Worrall Thompson and his products
go to www.awtonline.co.uk